POPULAR CARD GAMES

POPULAR CARD GAMES

BY

LAWRENCE H. DAWSON

AUTHOR OF
"A SHORT GUIDE TO CHESS,"
"DUPLICATE AUCTION & CONTRACT,"
"A GUIDE TO BACKGAMMON," ETC.

W. D. & H. O. WILLS
BRISTOL AND LONDON
BRANCH OF THE IMPERIAL TOBACCO CO.
(OF GREAT BRITAIN AND IRELAND), LTD.
1933

PRINTED IN GREAT BRITAIN

INTRODUCTION

ANY Introduction to a book with such a title as "Popular Card Games" might seem, at first sight, superfluous; but on second thoughts it has occurred to the author that a few lines might help the reader—if only by telling him just what he may expect to find within its covers—and what he may not!

Card games are legion, but POPULAR card games are not—consequently the author has not considered it his duty to write, or compile, an exhaustive treatise on everything that has been played with the "devil's picture-book"; nor has he attempted to play the part of the old law scribe and reproduce the official and invariably forbidding Laws that rigidly govern nearly all. What he has actually done is to imagine himself as one of a party of intelligent modern men and women who, when on a voyage to the latest Eldorado, have been shipwrecked on a not too inhospitable desert island with little saved from the wreck beside the purser's supply of cards for the voyage, and has then found that while all his fellow-sufferers know something of the general run of cards—how to deal, how to shuffle, how to "behave at table," and so on—none of them know all the popular games, and all of them want to! Luckily the voyage started just after the High and Mighty Ones had promulgated—let us hope finally—a new and almost perfect series of Laws for Contract and Auction; so he was able to include the gist of them, and here they are.

For the rest, the author has one word of caution to offer, and some acknowledgements to make. Firstly, in such universally popular games as POKER, VINGT-ET-UN, RUMMY, and one or two others, there are far more variations than room could be found for in any book not specially devoted to the particular game. Each locality, each "school," even, in a given locality, may have its special way of playing or of scoring points. So if his own pet variation does not here find a place, we trust that the reader, remembering the age-long impossibility of squeezing a quart into a pint pot, will be content to criticize us (if at all) on what we have given rather than on what we have been obliged to omit, and we hope also that he will find that with what we have given he will be able to test any variation as to its feasibility and, perchance, to invent new variations that will be in accordance with the general rules of any particular game.

Finally, acknowledgements are due, and are very gratefully given, to the many good friends and good card-players by whose advice and assistance the author has profited, and chiefly to J. T. Bolton, Esq., Chairman of the Press Club, who is mainly responsible for the whole of the Whist family (Auction, Contract, Whist and Solo), and to Major A. P. Le M. Sinkinson, O.B.E., of the Junior Naval and Military Club, who has kindly supervised the articles on the Bézique family and Piquet.

L.H.D.

THE PRESS CLUB,
LONDON, E.C. 4.
January, 1933.

CONTENTS

AUCTION BRIDGE

THOUGH the natural descent of Auction from Whist is traced directly through Bridge (a game which was exceedingly popular at the close of the last and in the early years of the present century) it is, in fact, an advance on Solo Whist, for in both there is an all-round-the-table auction to decide who shall play the hand. But in Auction Bridge there is this vital difference from Solo—the bidders in the auction specify the suit in which they propose to make the specified number of tricks, and also eventually decide the trump suit, or whether the hand shall be played with no trumps.

Two full packs of cards (52), each pack having backs of different colours, are used at Auction, and, as at Whist, there are four players, two of whom oppose the other two, partners remaining the same and sitting opposite each other during the whole of the rubber—which is the best of three games. Cutting for deal is effected in the usual way, and the original deal is taken by the player who cuts the lowest card, and is made one card at a time. After the first hand the deal goes round to the left, as at Whist.

A little detail with reference to the "making" of the cards may well be mentioned here. The partner of the player dealing should shuffle the other pack, and having done so place it to his right. When the first hand has been played, the player on the left of the original dealer takes up the second pack with his left hand and passes it over to the player on the right, who then cuts it. Due observance of this little formula will obviate the irritating but oft-asked question—"Whose deal next?"; also, it guards against the deal being made by the wrong hand. At certain stages, and in certain phases of the game, dealer is held to have a slight advantage at Auction; hence the necessity for keeping the deal right. A misdeal does not lose the deal, and the last card is not turned ; otherwise the preliminaries, including choice of seats, rank of cards in suits, etc., are as at Whist. For cutting, etc., the suits themselves rank according to their trick value, i.e., Spades (highest), Hearts, Diamonds and Clubs (lowest).

The object of the game is, firstly, to secure the Declaration, i.e., the privilege of playing the hands of oneself and partner (Dummy) by making the highest bid, for it is only the side that makes the highest bid that can score towards game ; and, secondly, to make at least as many tricks as are bid, going game if possible. The highest bid, whether undoubled, doubled, or redoubled is known as the "Contract." The "Book" for the Declarer is six tricks, all over this number count towards the fulfilment of the contract, and the value of the tricks—which varies according to the suit and which may be doubled and redoubled—is as in the Table on p. 13. The opponent's book is the difference between the final bid and seven (if the winning declaration is four Spades, for instance, opponent's book is three), and the value to them of any tricks over this is always the same, viz., 50 points each (100 if doubled, 200 if redoubled), which are entered as "honour" scores above the line and do not count towards game.

Bidding. The deal being completed the dealer has first bid and has many options, from the "pass" up to seven tricks over the book ("Grand Slam") either with a named suit for trump or with no trump. After the dealer the bidding goes on, round the table by the left until the last word has been said, that is, until three players have all "passed" and left the remaining player with the contract. Each bid must be an advance on a previous bid, in other words it must be of higher scoring value or, if of equal value, of a greater number of tricks. This law may be made clear by stating a case. If a call of two No Trumps has been made, totalling 20 points, three Diamonds (21), three Hearts (24), or three Spades (27) are sufficient as an overcall ; but it will need a call of four in Clubs to overcall, as three Clubs total only 18. Three Clubs, however, overcalls two

Spades, also totalling 18, because an extra trick is bid.

Here a word should be said on the subject of "Majority Calling," which for long divided Auction players into two camps, but which would seem to have been finally disposed of by the International Bridge Laws agreed and promulgated by the English, American and French authorities (Portland Club, Whist Club of New York and Commission Française du Bridge) towards the end of 1932. In Majority Calling a bid of a greater number of tricks outranked any bid of a less number, so that a call of five Clubs, for instance, value 30, took precedence of one of four No Trumps, value 40.

A bid may be doubled, but only by an opponent; and a doubled bid may be redoubled either by original caller or his partner. Doubling does not affect the value of the bid, and is annulled by a higher bid (thus a two Heart doubled is wiped out by a two Spade call); and there is no doubling of a redouble.

The partners making the highest bid are known as "Declarer" and "Dummy," the former (who plays the two hands) being he who originally named the suit (or No Trump) that becomes the winning declaration. As soon as the first card is led his partner spreads his cards face upwards on the table in front of him and becomes "Dummy." He takes no part in the play of that hand and is debarred from making suggestions or calling attention to errors, etc. He may not, for instance, warn his partner not to lead from the wrong hand, but he may, *if asked by his partner*, tell him in which hand the lead is.

In the event of all players passing during the auction there is a new deal by the next in turn to deal.

SCORING. Points for tricks made in the declared suit are scored below the line, and it requires 30 of such points to make game. Each trick over six counts:

6 points when Clubs are trumps
7 ,, when Diamonds are trumps
8 ,, when Hearts are trumps
9 ,, when Spades are trumps
10 ,, when there are No Trumps

Honours and other bonuses are scored above the line. There are five honours in a suit—the top five cards—and they are counted as follows :

With Trumps :

3 Honours	... ...	count	twice	the trick value
4 ,,	in the two hands	,,	4 times	,, ,, ,,
5 ,,	3 in one hand	,,	5 ,,	,, ,, ,,
4 ,,	in one hand	,,	8 ,,	,, ,, ,,
4 ,,	in one hand and the fifth in the other	,,	9 ,,	,, ,, ,,
5 ,,	in one hand	,,	10 ,,	,, ,, ,,

With No Trumps :

4 Aces in one hand	count	100	points
4 Aces between the two hands	,,	40	,,
3 Aces ,, ,, ,, ,,	,,	30	,,

100 points are scored above the line for Grand Slam (all thirteen tricks), 50 points for Little Slam (twelve tricks).

For each trick below the number it has been declared to make, the opponents score 50 points above the line. If Declarer is doubled and fulfils his contract he and his partner score 50 above the line, and 50 for each trick above the doubled call. These scores are multiplied by two in the event of a redouble—that is 100 per trick to opposition for each trick down, 100 to the Declarer for making the bid, and 100 for each trick over. The points under the line are also doubled and redoubled if a doubled or redoubled bid is played.

There is one detail with regard to the scoring that is not a matter of law but on which, nevertheless, too much stress cannot be laid, and that is that every player at a table should himself keep the score. The beginner at Auction will very quickly realize that as the game proceeds the state of the score below the line will have an increasing influence on the calling, and it is a breach of the etiquette of the game for a player to make an enquiry about the score during the process of bidding. No good Bridge player, therefore, will leave the scoring to his partner. Further, it is just as true to say that no one will ever become a good Bridge player until he has trained himself to keep the score in mind during the auction.

Synopsis of Scores for Auction Bridge

Tricks, Bonuses and Penalties	Un-dbld.	Dbld.	Re-dbld.
Points per trick			
Clubs ...	6	12	24
Diamonds ...	7	14	28
Hearts ...	8	16	32
Spades ...	9	18	36
No Trumps ...	10	20	40
Bonuses			
Making Contract	—	50	100
Overtricks (each)	—	50	100
Penalties			
Each Under-trick	50	100	200

Required for Game	30
Slams	
Little Slam	50
Grand Slam	100
Rubber Points	250

HONOURS	
With No Trumps	
4 Aces in one hand ...	100
4 Aces divided	40
3 Aces ...	30
With Trumps	times the value of the trump suit
5 in one hand	10
4 in one and 1 in the other...	8
4 in one and 0 in the other...	8
5 divided, 3 and 2 ...	5
4 divided ...	4
3	2

Note. The score for Honours is unaffected by doubling or redoubling.

One or two laws of the game may here be given.

There should always be a new deal if at any time during the deal a card is exposed. It is impossible to determine, during the deal, what value an exposed card may eventually possess; this, therefore, is the only safe procedure, whatever the apparent value of the exposed card—high or low.

If a player makes a bid out of turn other than a pass, and either opponent notices the irregularity, the player on the left of the offender may demand a new deal. If a new deal is not demanded the out of turn call stands, and the auction goes on as if nothing untoward had happened.

If a player bids an insufficient number of tricks in a suit to overbid a previous call, the player on the left may allow it to stand, or may elect to have the call amended to the requisite number of tricks. In the latter case the offender's partner must be silent for the rest of the auction for that hand unless an opponent overbids or doubles. An alternative penalty for the overbid is the closing of the auction, in which case the last bid previous to the irregular one stands.

If, in the course of the auction, a player, by a slip of the tongue, names a suit which he did not intend to mention, or in any other way makes an unintentional bid he is allowed to correct it in the same breath, and no penalty is exacted.

Just a further, if somewhat elementary word concerning the auction, which can be by way of the simplest of illustrations.

A bid of one, two, or three, etc., is a declaration on the part of the caller that he contracts, with the assistance of such cards as his partner may possess, to make the stated tricks in addition to the book (six) with a named suit trumps, or in No Trumps as the case may be.

The functions fulfilled in the making of a bid are three, and, though there are people who would be dogmatic as to the relative importance of the three, perhaps it is safer to link them together. These functions are :

To give information concerning the hand.
To obtain the right of playing the hand.
To prevent the opposition from bidding.

One objective in bidding being to give information to the partner, the fact that Bridge differs from Whist in being a twenty-six card game for the two players instead of a thirteen card game for one player must ever be borne in mind. Most emphatically is Auction Bridge a partnership game, with trouble for the selfish player who calls irrespective of anything his partner may say, and who (by implication at any rate) is actuated by a selfish desire to play the hand.

Opening Bids. There would be immediate disagreement even among experienced players if an attempt were made to lay down strict conventions in regard to what holdings justify a bid, and what cards do not. But even though the experts may not agree as to what exactly constitutes, for instance, an "opening bid," some general observations may be made, and some hints given, concerning bidding which is justified by particular holdings. So let us start with the first, or opening, bid—that of the dealer.

Any information which is given right at the start—given for the benefit of the partner, of course—should be reliable information ; that is, there must be tricks in the hand to justify an original bid, and by tricks is meant "quick tricks," not problematical tricks which depend upon the ultimate establishment of a long suit devoid of master cards.

In some schools an original bid of one in a four-card suit headed by Ace, K, and with some useful outside cards, is deprecated. Actually, however, little harm can come from such a bid, though a five-card suit headed by the Ace, K makes, of course, for greater safety. Here is a typical hand which justifies an opening bid of one Spade :

AN OPENING BID OF ONE SPADE

And here is a hand on which, generally speaking and in the absence of any need for heroics, the first caller should pass :

FIRST CALLER SHOULD PASS

The hand at the foot of the previous page looks good; but a bid would convey false information to a partner; and, in any case, it is a hand on which it may be well to wait for developments. Remember that the second chance to bid almost invariably comes.

No hard and fast rule can be laid down concerning an original call of one No Trump, but a hand of this type can be regarded as about the minimum:

A MINIMUM NO TRUMP CALL

It is generally conceded that the call of one No Trump is advisable when it can be made legitimately and originally. Consider what impression would be conveyed to the partner if the holder of the hand given above were to pass; he would have no indication that something could be expected from it and so, in all probability, would be a little less adventurous in bidding than he would be if he knew that the first caller had some useful supporting cards.

The second caller is very much in the position of the first. On him is the same onus of giving original reliable information to his partner. Third caller—that is the partner of the original Declarer—has other points to consider, viz., the bids which have preceded him, possibly one from his partner and one from his opponent. Third caller's holding—and fourth caller's as well in due course—must be looked at in conjunction, first of all, with his partner's original call. Very real steps towards efficiency at this game can be made if the habit is cultivated of trying to visualize, from the bidding, the cards held both by partner and by opponent.

Third caller—and fourth also—with good cards, and support for partner's suit, say three to the Q—should put his partner up in that suit, if there has been an intervening call. It should not be forgotten that one objective of the bid is to arrive at the best possible suit—or it may be No Trumps—in which the hands of the partners should be played.

A few further observations regarding the auction may prove helpful. It can be stated, as a rough principle, that more rubbers are lost by under-bidding than by over-bidding. " Sitting on the fence " is a type of play which many devotees of Auction seem to like, but such an attitude, in an ordinary situation, does not pay. Good cards are given to players for the purpose of bidding, for making tricks which go down to your own score, rather than for causing opponents to fail in their bids. The game and rubber can only be won on bids made.

As, in the absence of any opposing bids, game can be made on a good hand from a score of love even when a bid of only one in a suit is made, there are many players who do not realize the importance of calling more than one unless forced to do so. " You can always go up," is a stock remark. Sometimes, as will be found from experience, it is the opponents who go up, or who, as the result of the call of one originally, manage to force such a caller " out of his depth."

By calling more than one of a suit, when the hand justifies it, the wings of the opposition are clipped considerably. Here is a hand which, logically, justifies a two bid of Spades even as a start :

A BID OF TWO SPADES

Somewhere in the other three hands there are clearly a lot of Hearts, since the bidder has only one of that suit. By a bid of two Spades, the bidder first of all tells his partner that there is a fair prospect of making a lot of tricks if Spades are trumps, and in the second place *three* Hearts must be bid to overcall the two Spades. It may well happen that the player immediately behind the original caller could have called *two* Hearts, and that his partner could in due course support that suit. But neither of the partners' hands justifies a three-Heart bid. So the original bid of two has prevented them from talking to each other about their hands. Something attempted, something achieved! This idea—it can scarcely be called a principle—may very simply be explained by asking the question; "Why start with a bid of one in a suit if prepared to go to two or three, even without support from his partner, when pushed by the opposition?" And the answer is, "To prevent the opposition from pushing."

It is a Bridge axiom about which there is no question that, except as sheer bluff—which is not Bridge at all but Poker—there must not be a No Trump call over a suit which is not held by the No Trump caller. There are good players, however, who think that, especially when the partner has shown strength somewhere, it is good policy to call No Trumps over a suit with two "stoppers" in that suit even if the other cards in the hand are not good. The call of No Trumps over a suit bid, when the suit is held, says to the player's partner in so many words, "Don't be afraid of this suit." By the players who adopt this line of reasoning it is held that thus calling No Trumps over the suit bid they are not telling their partner that they have a good all-round hand, but merely that they hold the suit called immediately in front of them.

Doubling. The bidding having gone forward, players will presently begin to wonder whether the time has not come to stop the effort to make a call and begin the effort to get points from the opposition. This is when the "double" comes in as a bid.

Just when to double is not an easy question, except in those cases when the opposition is clearly "flag-flying"—that is, trying, as a kind of forlorn hope, to keep the rubber alive. As a first and sound policy, *be wary of doubling the opponents into a game bid.* Suppose, without any score towards game, the opponents have gone three Hearts, and are prepared to leave it at that. The double may look good, but don't double unless it is a "stone-waller." The three Hearts, if made, would not give the opponents game; but if by chance—which is merely another word for good play—or by an exceptional distribution of the cards the opponents make their three Hearts then they have incidentally been made the present of the game and possibly the rubber, with its bonus of 300 points—250 for the rubber and 50 for making the doubled bid.

Many a bid has been made too, on the information which is conveyed by a player doubling a call. The play of the Declarer will be influenced by the position of the opponent who has doubled. Suppose, as a simple example, a player holds K, J, 9 and a small one of a suit which has been called by the player on his left, The double is made. The good player will immediately "place" these cards in the hand of the "doubler" and make the necessary finesses in the trump suit—that is avail himself of information which the double has given. The calling in general should influence the double.

Also, in respect of a double, there has crept into the game a phrase which should not really have a part in it, viz., "free double." What is meant by it is that if the opponents have made a call on which they are likely to go to game anyway, there can be little harm in a "chance it" double. But the possibility of a redouble is always present, and when a redoubled call is made the doubler may realize that his double wasn't "free" by any means!

Another point about the double is that it may prove a two-edged weapon. The opponents may have a sound "switch" (or alternative) call, one which they can make; and they will begin to think about this when the double is forthcoming. As a good line of play the following may be commended; when the opponents are in the position in which you want them, leave them there.

Another axiom ; don't double one suit unless prepared to double any other suit to which a switch may be made. This seems a hard saying, but it is very excellent advice.

At any time during the auction any player at the table may request to have the whole of the calls, from the start, repeated, but after the auction is over this privilege ceases. No player may ask questions concerning the calls after the auction has closed. When this stage is reached there remains the playing of the hand.

THE PLAY. The player who has to play the hand is the first Declarer of the suit in which it is finally played, as we have already seen. Thus, if A has originally called Spades, and the hand is played in Spades, A will play the hand and his partner B will be Dummy, putting his hand down on the table when the player on Declarer's left has led his first card to the first trick.

The word Dummy means what it says, though goodness knows plenty of Dummies take a long time to get accustomed to their temporary rôle. To what we have said above apropos the very small extent of his powers we have only to add that he may ask his partner if he is void of a suit which he has either trumped or on which he has discarded, but if he does so after he has seen any cards still held by the opponents his partner may not withdraw his card. Also, he may take part in any discussions concerning the score or on questions of fact and law. He cannot himself revoke.

If a player fails to correct a revoke before the trick is turned and quitted, the offender and his partner cannot score any points save honours, and one hundred points are added to the opponents' score. If the Declarer is not the revoking party he may elect to take two of his opponents' tricks, which then count as tricks he himself has made, instead of the 100 points.

If a revoke by the opponents of the Declarer is corrected before the trick is turned and quitted, the card played in error can be treated as an exposed card, and called when desired ; or Declarer can claim that the card to be played shall be the highest or lowest which the offender holds in the proper suit.

THE DECLARER'S LEAD. In considering the play of the hand, the Declarer—that is the player who plays both his own hand and that of Dummy—has two considerations to bear in mind. First the making of the "bid," and second, the possibility of making such over-tricks as will give his side game.

It cannot be too strongly emphasized that the most opportune time to give consideration to the combined hands is at the moment when the first lead is made. A little thought then will save a lot of thought later on, and possibly save tricks as well. Consider the plan of campaign right from the start; weigh up the possibilities of the two hands, and play accordingly. For instance, Dummy's hand must be looked at in the light of re-entry cards, the necessity or otherwise of making certain finesses, and the possibility of using Dummy to make tricks with cards on which the Declarer himself can throw away losers.

In addition to this, there is the decision to be made as to what the player making the lead is leading from. For instance, few good players as a first lead which is "blind," and without information from a partner, lead away from the King. If there is a lead of a small card from a suit in which Dummy has length and certain strength—say Ace, Q to six, the finesse of the Q is doubtful play, as there is the probability that the original lead was a singleton. In this case if third hand held the K a return of the lead would enable the original leader to make a small trump.

THE LEAD AGAINST THE DECLARER. The play of the hands against the Declarer is, however, likely to be more complicated. It frequently happens that the original leader has had some indication from his partner concerning a suit. In this case the original leader has a clear course, the generally accepted formula being the highest of the partner's suit if three or fewer cards are held, and the fourth highest if four or more are held in that suit.

The lead of the partner's suit is the safest possible opening in the absence of any necessity for showing the partner another strong suit or one which, for some reason, it is expected he will return. After the first lead, the rest of the leads against the Declarer become easier, and in this connection there is a well-known formula which has stood the test of time; lead through strength and up to weakness. Suppose Dummy has an Ace, Q, 9 suit displayed on the table, and the player on his right has the lead. To lead that suit would be leading through strength—correct play. After all, if the Declarer has the intervening cards the two of them (Declarer and Dummy) are going to make the tricks in that suit, but it is at least possible that the intervening cards are held by the leader's partner. On the other hand, if the player furthest away from Dummy has the lead he can lead up to weakness, as the Declarer will then have to play between first and second opponent.

In the absence of any other information, and also in the absence of a really strong suit, quite a good lead is top of a sequence, and in this connection a word of advice should be offered. Don't play false cards to a partner. Take for instance, the lead of the Q from a Q, J, 10 suit through Dummy. If Dummy has the K and it is put up, third player may take it with the Ace. If Dummy has no high card the third player has at least gained some information from the lead of the Q by his partner. He knows that his partner has the essential cards to back up this suit.

What is called a "free look" at Dummy can sometimes be had by the original leader who has no information from his partner. Take this hand with Hearts as trumps. Original leader holds:

A "FREE LOOK"

The lead of the K of Spades, which would take the trick and also show the partner that the Ace is behind it, would enable the leader to have a "free look" at Dummy. And after the free look the plan of attack can be framed partly in accord with Dummy's holding.

The importance of not playing false cards, save on exceptional occasions, should be realized. The partner leads the small card of a suit. A small one is played by Dummy. Third hand holds J, 10, 9. The 9 should be played. The only occasion when a false card should be played is when it is advisable deliberately to deceive the opposition. Suppose fourth player has only K and Q of a suit. It may pay to play the K to take the trick as, on the next lead, the opponent may think that the Q is in the hand on his right and finesse.

In the playing of the hand by the partners who are against Dummy certain points need to be watched. For instance, if Dummy has only two small trumps and is short in some suit, it often happens that the Declarer will make the attempt to use the small trumps on the short suits. A lead of trumps by either of the partners in such case is usually a wise move. The Declarer will often reveal his intention to use the small trumps very early in the hand.

As a rule too, it is bad play to allow the Declarer to trump in one hand and discard in the other; this, of course, happens when a suit is led of which both the Declarer and the Dummy are short. But don't be afraid of leading so as to compel Declarer to trump out of his strong trump hand so long as there are losing cards of that suit in Dummy. Peg away; weaken the hand which is strong in trumps! That long suit may come in very useful at the later stages of the hand.

When partners are playing against the Declarer there is a recognized signal from one to the other which is well understood and often used. Suppose that A, with the lead, holds Ace, K to five of a suit, and his partner has only two—the 8 and the 6. The partner will throw the 8 on the first lead, and this is a signal in the first place to continue the suit. At the second lead, when the

6 is played, the indication should be as clear as daylight that the partner has no more of that suit, and that he wants to trump a master in it still held by the opposition. " Petering " is the technical term for the signal.

It is also necessary to make the effort, from time to time, to take out certain re-entry cards in Dummy. Suppose he holds the Ace, K, Q and three others of a non-trump suit with an outside Ace and is weak in trumps. The effort to take out the outside Ace before the trumps are exhausted is worth while, as it prevents Declarer from using the long suit when trumps are all gone.

CONTRACT BRIDGE

THAT CONTRACT BRIDGE is becoming increasingly popular is a fact beyond all argument. Just to what extent, and how quickly, it will take the place of Auction Bridge need not be argued here. Contract Bridge in something like its present form came to us from America, and there came with it such talk of conventions, of fancy bidding, "psychic" calls, of this system and that system, that the game started some distance behind scratch. There were many points about it which, at first, seemed to offend British traditions concerning card games. Many people were frightened of it, especially those who gathered their information as to what the game really was from those who themselves knew little about it.

It is likely that all the incidental and ill-informed talk with which the game was associated prevented it from taking hold as quickly as it otherwise would have done—but the grip is there all right. Contract Bridge appeals particularly to those people who, rightly or wrongly, consider that they have in them the makings of good card players; and the game, properly played, is essentially one for good card players.

Just as Auction Bridge was a natural advance on Bridge, so does Contract Bridge carry the advance, if the phrase may be used, to the logical conclusion. It is in the logical-conclusion sense that we find the chief difference between Contract Bridge and Auction Bridge. In Auction Bridge it is possible to make a game without calling a game. Four Spades made when only one is called still wins a game of Auction from a love score. In Contract Bridge points can only be scored towards the making of game to the extent to which a contract has been entered into. Bonus points are, of course, scored above the line for over-tricks in contracts, but the first big feature is that a game cannot be scored at Contract unless a game is called. This fact, as will be seen later, has a real influence on the calling in general.

SCORING. There are two other important factors. One is that the scoring is changed, in certain particulars, when one side have a game to their credit. They are then described as "Vulnerable," while those without a game are "Non-vulnerable." It would be interesting to know how many potential Contract players have been put off by hearing these terrible-sounding words associated with the game, but apparently they are the best that can be found, so they must be used here.

The other important factor is that the scoring in Contract Bridge has been so arranged that there is an incentive to bid for Slams—Small Slam or Big Slam—and that incentive is in the shape of a very substantial bonus. This inducement to bid for Slams is the last word in the logical conclusion to which reference has been made above.

A new code of Laws of Contract, drawn up by the same International Board as that responsible for the Laws of Auction (see p. 11), and a system of scoring new in many particulars, has recently been agreed upon. The up-to-date method of counting the score should be mastered by all players at the outset or, if this is not possible, should at least be kept at hand for reference. The scoring is not really so complicated as appears at first glance, and regular players soon find it is quite unnecessary for them to refer to the table. It should be stated that a game consists of a minimum of 100 points and the points to be scored are given below.

THE SCORING AT CONTRACT

TRICK SCORE

For each odd trick bid and made

In Clubs or Diamonds	20
In Hearts or Spades	30
In No Trumps, 1st, 3rd, 5th and 7th ...	30
In No Trumps, 2nd, 4th and 6th ...	40

These points are doubled in the case of a doubled contract, and are quadrupled in the case of a redoubled contract.

Premium Score

For each overtrick a premium equal to the trick value

When doubled and not Vulnerable ... 100

When doubled and Vulnerable 200

Both these points are doubled in the case of a redoubled contract.

Undertrick Penalties

	When not Vulnerable.			When Vulnerable.		
	Undbld.	Dbld.	Redbld.	Undbld.	Dbld.	Redbld.
First ...	50	100	200	100	200	400
Second ...	50	150	300	150	300	600
Third ...	50	200	400	200	400	800

and so on with penalties at the same rate of progression for further undertricks.

Majority Calling (see p. 11) is the universal rule at Contract. This means, of course, that an increased number of odd tricks contracted for outbids any smaller number, i.e., three of any other suit (or No Trumps) overbids two of any other suit, and so on. It should be added, for the sake of regularity, that the suits rank in the same order as in Auction—Clubs, Diamonds, Hearts, Spades and then No Trumps.

It will be seen from the scoring table (see next page), that from a love score, game can be made only by a call of five in Clubs or Diamonds—four in Hearts or Spades and three in No Trumps. Just one little peculiarity about the No Trump reckoning—an innovation this—should be noticed. The odd trick in No Trumps counts 30, the second trick counts 40, the third 30 and the fourth 40 and so on alternately. Previously the scoring in No Trumps was 35 per trick, and the alteration was apparently made with the object of cutting the inconvenient fives out of the score-sheet. This change has, however, made a slight and possibly un-anticipated difference. If by chance a game is now built up by means of single No Trump calls it would require four such calls to make a game, whereas a bid of one No Trumps made (30) plus a bid of two No Trumps made (30 and 40) reckon up to a game. A single call of three No Trumps also scores game.

SYNOPSIS OF SCORES FOR CONTRACT BRIDGE

TRICKS	Trick Score		
	Undbld	Doubled	Redoubled
Each odd trick bid and made in			
Clubs or Diamonds ...	20	40	80
Hearts or Spades ...	30	60	120
No Trumps, 1st, 3rd, 5th and 7th	30	60	120
2nd, 4th and 6th ...	40	80	160

BONUSES	Premium Score					
	Not Vulnerable			Vulnerable		
	Un-dbld	Dbld	Re-dbld	Un-dbld	Dbld	Re-dbld
Each Overtrick ...	Trick Value	100	200	Trick Value	200	400
Undertrick Penalties						
First	50	100	200	100	200	400
Second	50	150	300	150	300	600
Third	50	200	400	200	400	800
Fourth	50	250	500	250	500	1000
Fifth	50	300	600	300	600	1200
Sixth	50	350	700	350	700	1400
Seventh	50	400	800	400	800	1600

Slams	Not Vulnerable	Vulnerable
Little Slam bid and made	500	750
Grand Slam bid and made	1500	2250

Honours

With Trumps ...	Four Honours in One Hand	100
,, ...	Five Honours in One Hand	150
With No Trumps	Four Aces in One Hand ...	150

Required for Game 100

Rubber Points

For three-game rubber	500
For two-game rubber	700
For unfinished rubber—for one game	300

There is no bonus at all for Slams made unless they are bid, but provided they are bid the bonus is worth having. Look at this :

	Not Vulnerable	Vulnerable
For Little Slam bid and made	500 pts.	750 pts.
For Grand, or Big Slam—bid and made	1,500 ,,	2,250 ,,

It should also be noted—for this is another recent change—that there is no special bonus above the line for the making of a doubled or redoubled contract, but there is a substantial rubber-winning bonus. When the rubber is won in two games—that is without the opponents making a game and thereby becoming Vulnerable—the rubber points are 700, and in a three-game rubber the rubber points are 500.

Honours are more easily counted in Contract than in Auction, for here the holding of honours is a matter for one hand only ; honour holding in the joint hands has no significance in Contract, and fewer honours than the following do not score at all.

Four honours in one hand of any suit in which the hand is played count 100 points. Five honours of trump suit in one hand, 150 points. Four Aces in one hand when no trumps, 150 points.

The Laws of Contract. Having got the scoring system " off our chests," it is now necessary to refer to certain Laws of the game ; partly because some of them are new and not properly understood, and partly because some of the agreed Laws of Contract are different from those of Auction Bridge. It has only to be mentioned that the present Laws are the outcome of three years of discussion by the " International Board " to make it clear that they should be known and, what is more important, should be obeyed. Of Contract it can be said, with truth, that it is the most likely of all card games to impress on players the great importance of playing according to rule, and also the most likely to remove that ridiculous feeling which many card players have harboured all their lives—that the people who insist on playing a game of cards according to rule are not nice to know.

The procedure in the cut for partners is interesting and unusual. Ace has become the highest card in a cut, and the two players with the highest cards are partners, while the player drawing the highest card has the deal and the choice of seats. This is almost a complete reversal of the old form of cutting for partners and choice of seats.

Touching a card of the exposed hand, by the Declarer—that is the player playing the hand—now has exactly the same effect as actually playing the card. If the Declarer touches any card in Dummy, except for the purpose of arranging such card—which purpose must be announced—that card is played, even though it is not covered.

Another important point of procedure concerns the Declarer playing from the wrong hand. If he plays from the wrong hand—either from his own when it is Dummy's lead or vice versa—either of the opponents may demand that he leads from the correct hand, and if either exercises this right then, if the correct hand has a card of the suit that has been wrongly played, that suit can be insisted upon. To make this provision clear; if Declarer touches the Seven of Hearts in Dummy, as if to lead, when the lead was in the Declarer's own hand, the Declarer can be asked to lead Hearts from his own hand. In the opinion of most people this provision—which has been an American Law for some time—was much over-due in England. All of us know the player who considers himself capable of playing his own hand and that of Dummy well, but who seems utterly incapable of keeping a mental note of the hand in which the previous trick was taken! Incidentally, of course, the player who, by leading out of a wrong hand occasionally received information about the position of the cards, has been scotched.

The Revoke. Most interesting of these Contract Laws perhaps—and certainly illustrative of the thought which has been put into them—are those relating to the Revoke. These regulations really must be mastered. In the first place there is now only one penalty—

no alternative. For the first established revoke in a hand two tricks made by the revoking side go to the other side for the final count-up. For each revoke after the first one by the same pair in the same hand, one trick goes to the other side.

Note this revoke point. Tricks made before the revoke cannot be taken away in any circumstances. Here is an illustration. The contract is Four Hearts. The Declarer makes the first ten tricks—that is his contract. Then, if he revokes at the eleventh trick he has still made his contract: the two tricks cannot be taken from his ten. The same is true of the other side. If, playing against a contract of Four Hearts, the opponents make four tricks—putting the contract down—before one or other revokes, they have still put the contract down, and the two tricks penalty cannot be enforced against them in respect of these tricks won. Once more, to make the matter perfectly clear, *there can be no interference with the tricks made before the revoke.*

One other revoke point. There is no penalty for a revoke after the eleventh trick of the hand. These regulations make clear that it has become necessary to remember on which trick an established revoke occurred. To say that this revoke rule may give rise to argument is merely to state the obvious. The object here, however, is not to argue but to put readers in possession of the Law on this matter.

One argument which has been raised against the Revoke Laws should be dealt with here, because in doing so another point can be cleared up. It is suggested that under the new Laws it is possible for a wily player—a cheat if you like—to revoke to his own advantage. Let it be noted that even the Contract legislators thought of this, for they state officially ; " The Laws are not designed to prevent dishonourable practices : consequently there are no penalties to cover intentional violations " of the Laws or of the etiquette of the game. " Ostracism," they say, " is the ultimate remedy where intentional offences are repeated."

There may be wonderment as to whether all the

points which are set down in respect of what is called the etiquette of the game will be observed. Some of them may be stated here, however, for the benefit of those who, unintentionally, but none the less certainly, have transgressed in the past, and have no desire to transgress in the future. Here are the more important Contract Bridge " Commandments " on the etiquette of the game—the things " not done ":

Calling in any pointed manner, as with special inflection, intonation or emphasis.

Showing unnecessary haste, nervousness or delay in passing, doubling, etc.

Making any unnecessary request for a review of the calls so far made in the auction, or unnecessarily asking that the cards played to a trick should be placed.

In any way drawing attention to the score except for one's own necessary information.

Giving by word, manner or act any indication of the nature of one's hand, or making any remark, question, or gesture from which an inference might be drawn.

Calling attention to the number of tricks needed to complete or defeat the contract, or to the fact that it has already been fulfilled.

Indicating in any way approval or disapproval of one's partner's call or play.

Undue delay in playing to a trick when the play does not call for special consideration.

We have already alluded to the conventions which have been, and are, associated with the game, and as something more will be said of them later, here is a point worthy of notice. A " convention " may be defined in brief as " any method of conveying information by the play of the cards which would not be understood by the uninitiated " ; and it is forbidden to use any convention in calling which has not been announced for the benefit of all the players at the table.

It is not possible to give here a complete list of the Laws—either old or new—of Contract Bridge. They are almost a book in themselves. One general principle in regard to irregularities in the calling should, however, be mentioned, for the question as to which opponent shall decide whether there shall be a new deal or the enforcement of a penalty in the event of an irregularity now no longer arises. The opponent on the left of the "guilty" player must make the decision "on his own," and without consultation with his partner.

Observation inspires—indeed practically compels—the assertion that thousands of people who think they are playing Contract are, in fact, only playing at playing it—their actual game being merely ordinary Auction, with the sole difference that the score is reckoned in the Contract way; that is, they insist on a game call being made before a game can be counted. The building up of Little Slam and Big Slam bids has no place in the calculations of such people.

It is not our purpose to take away from these people any of the enjoyment which they get out of playing the game of Contract *à la* Auction Bridge—or more accurately still, *Plafond*. Provision can scarcely be made, however, for players who refuse to go the whole Contract hog, and it must be accepted as a premise that the suggestions on Contract Bridge procedure which follow are intended for those who wish to play the game in its complete sense; that is, to play Contract Bridge under the Official Laws and with a view to getting the extreme value out of the hands which fate allots them.

It is because of the necessity, in the first place, of bidding with a view to a game, and of the necessity of bidding, in the second place, with a possible view to a Slam of one kind or the other, that calls should convey accurate information. This point has already been made in respect of Auction Bridge; it is ten times more important in respect of Contract. Scarcely anything save calamity can befall two partners at this game unless, in the conversations which they hold with each other—that is, in the calls they make—the truth is told.

QUICK TRICKS. The preceding paragraph can be summed up in a different way by saying that first calls must, for the purpose of getting the best out of the combined hands held by the partners, be based on quick tricks. Hence the importance of getting a clear idea, at a very early stage in the learning of the game, of what the expression "quick tricks" means. A "quick trick" is a card that will win on the first or second round, therefore honours are the only cards which count in reckoning them.

Ace of any suit is an obvious quick trick. Ace, K of the same suit mean two quick tricks; and K and Q of a suit, with a small card, count as one quick trick. Strictly speaking there are no others; but there are certain combinations of cards, as will be explained later, which are worth reckoning as half-tricks, and which will enter into consideration in the calling.

So that the quick trick idea may be mastered in stages, consider this holding:

QUICK TRICKS

This hand contains four quick tricks—two for the Ace, K suit, one for the Ace suit, and one for the K, Q suit. It is given solely as an elementary lesson in the counting of quick tricks. Not the slightest harm could really come of an original bid of one Heart on such a hand. As a matter of fact it contains more quick tricks than are generally considered necessary for an original call. By some players—the very cautious—it is held that there must be three in a hand to justify an original bid, while others—of a more adventurous nature—think that two-and-a-half quick tricks are sufficient to justify an original call provided that there are honours, and at least four—preferably five—cards of the suit called.

The use of the phrase "half tricks" calls for explanation. King at least once guarded in a suit may be reckoned as a half trick ; so can Q, J and another in the same suit. Certain holdings in the same suit can be reckoned up together in computing the tricks in a hand. For example, Ace, Q of the same suit reckon one-and-a-half quick tricks ; so do Ace, J, 10, also K, Q, 10.

It will be realised that these quick-trick reckonings are based on the well-justified expectation that the cards will make tricks even when defending against a call. A snag in the quick-trick reckoning may be mentioned. Ace, K, Q of the same suit do not, for the purpose of quick tricks, count as three, though they may rightly be counted as two-and-a-half, or two-and-a-plus, as some players phrase it.

The object of these notes concerning quick tricks should be realised. The original caller does not know what cards are held either by the opponents or by his partner. But the partner may have such cards in his hand that, accepting the information originally given as truthful, he can read, fairly accurately, what the original caller holds, and proceed with the bidding accordingly.

As a good line of argument, which will be appreciated by Auction Bridge players, it can be suggested that what is put forward as an *idea* in calling at Auction should be *more than an idea* in Contract—it is a statement to the effect that with average support from the partner, the call can be duly made. This suggestion is obviously on the " play safe " lines, and is not put down for general acceptance in all circumstances. The circumstances naturally demand variation in the calling from time to time, but for the moment the idea is being kept in mind that telling the truth for a start is the surest way to the building up of a sound game call, or alternatively of a Slam bid.

In the event of a pass by first player, second player may safely call on a quick-trick holding as previously explained. It is generally agreed that third caller, to justify an original call after two players have passed, must be slightly stronger than caller number one or two, and that fourth hand, to open the calling, must be even stronger still.

In actual play there are more hands thrown in—that is without a bid at all—at Contract Bridge than at Auction. It is frequently shown, when hands have been thrown in and there is talk of what the players held, that if either of the partners had started the bidding a game call, even from a love score, could have been built up. There should be no undue worry on this account. There is some truth in the observation that the better the players the more frequently will the hands be thrown in. Better two hands which would have made quite a good trick-winning combination thrown in, than calling which is not justified on the quick-trick reckoning. The foregoing is not an attempt to lay down a convention; it is just a commonsense view-point. The convention part of Contract Bridge will have its place in these notes in due time.

As an accepted formula for the bidding of one No Trump the holding should be two-and-a-half or possibly three honour tricks spread over three suits. Experience suggests, however, that the bidding of a suit, if fairly solid and fairly long, is a safer mode of procedure for a start. The No Trumps call can often better be built up by partners if the original caller declares his good suit.

A natural question will arise as to how information should be given concerning a hand in which the suits are not so evenly divided. Take the case of a hand like this :

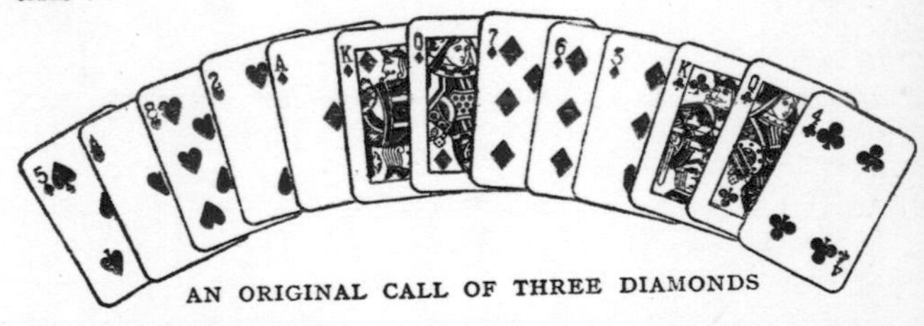

AN ORIGINAL CALL OF THREE DIAMONDS

The original caller on such a hand may well call three Diamonds, conveying to the partner complete command and solidity in the Diamond suit—in which he has six tricks if played in that suit or in No Trumps—and three other quick tricks. That is nine tricks in all. The reason for the call of Three in the Diamond suit, rather than Two, will be given, and in giving it we come inevitably to deal with conventions.

CONVENTIONS. Whether conventions—apart from the simple one of telling the truth—are an absolute necessity in Contract Bridge, may be arguable. But certain of the popular and oft-played conventions must be mentioned, as they are definitely a part of the game as now being played.

THE " FORCING TWO " BID. One of these conventions is called the " forcing two." It is given this title because after a bid by the original caller of two in a suit, which is not a game, the partner is " forced " to make a bid of some kind. Here is a hand on which a forcing two would be called when partners were adopting this convention :

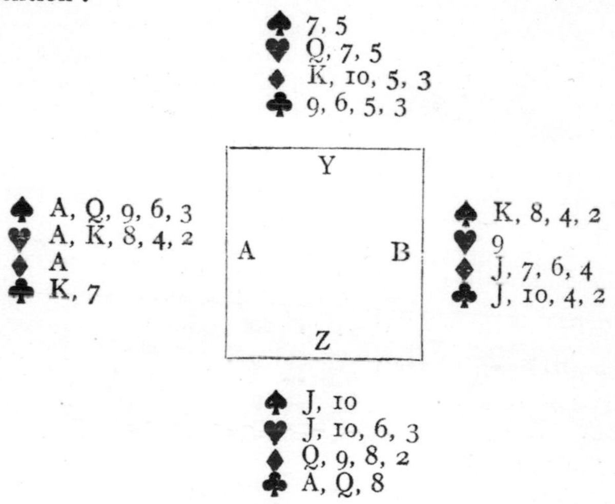

A is dealer and reckoning up his honour tricks to five—the considered minimum for a forcing two—calls two Hearts. Y passes, and B, having no quick tricks, says two No Trumps. Z can only pass. A must not leave his partner's call in—obviously—but the bidding being open he has another try—and calls three Spades. This call changes the partner's view-point. With his four Spades to the K he can put up A to four Spades and there the call stays—and is made. The question of bidding a Slam by A and B on this holding ceased to arise when B said that he had very little in his hand.

The point which will immediately occur to those who are merely thinking casually about this convention will be somewhat to the following effect—what is the use of calling two No Trumps with nothing in the hand, and thus compelling the original caller to go higher than he did in the first instance? The question is a sensible one, and there is a sensible answer given by those who play this convention. When the original caller announced, as he did by the two call, that he had five (possibly five-and-a-half) quick tricks, he knew nothing of his partner's holding. He was telling him about the number of tricks held, so that if the partner's hand also had strength, the building up of a game call from love, or even a Slam, would proceed. Thus we come back to what was previously stated, that the bidding has for its object the making of a game score or, alternatively, of a Slam, Big or Little.

Any real response from the partner to the forcing two—that is other than the purely negative two No Trumps—would convey to the original caller that his partner had tricks in his hand. Two-and-a-half is considered, by most players of this convention, to be a sound put up.

THE "JUMP" BID. How is the partner of the original caller to show exceptional strength in his own hand—that is, such strength as will suggest the possibility of a Slam? The answer to this is—by what is known as the "jump" bid, i.e., a raise of more than one.

Here—and running the risk of being accused of repetition—the sheer necessity for keeping the score in mind should once more be insisted upon. Consider the tragedies which may arise from non-compliance with this elementary principle. The original caller bids a Spade when his side's score below the line stands at sixty. One Spade does not give the side a game, but two Spades would do so. The partner, not watching the score, makes a jump bid to three Spades, having the sort of hand which he thinks can work up to a four Spade bid, but not to a Slam. The jump bid which takes the pair over a game bid will immediately be construed by the original caller as an invitation to go for a Slam, and indication that there is exceptional strength (beyond what is actually there) in the partner's hand. And caller number one, assuming, as he must, that his partner knows the score, immediately goes out for the Slam. The jump bid—that is a raise of two or more—is a Slam invitation.

Here is a typical complete hand, giving the holding of all the four players, on which a Small Slam bid is safe. The cards were actually held, as shown, in the International Contract Bridge test between England and America.

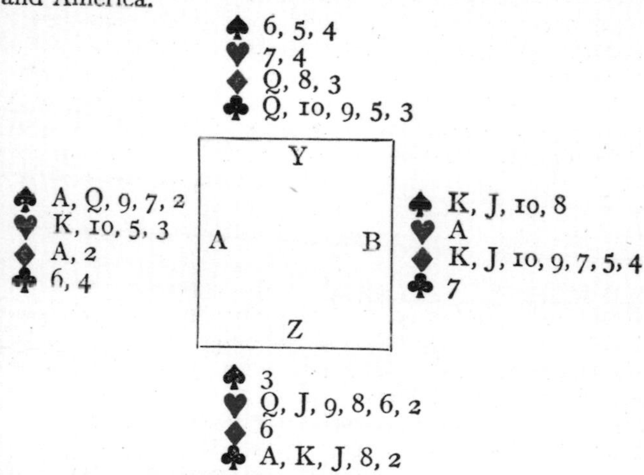

Consider how a very sound Small Slam can be bid. A, the dealer, calls an original Spade, and it will be noted that he has three quick tricks, reckoning the Aces as two, the Ace, Q suit as another half trick, and the K of Hearts as yet another half. There is no call from Y. Now B, looking at his hand, considers what A can hold. He has at least five Spades, which means that in any case the four held by B should enable all the trumps to be drawn. As B possesses the Ace of Hearts, A's other trick must be the Ace, either of Diamonds or of Clubs, with probably the K of Hearts outside. B thereupon calls three Diamonds, showing the two-and-a-half quick tricks, and also "jumping," as previously explained in connection with this convention. A, possessing the Ace of Diamonds, then knows that B must have the Ace either of Clubs or of Hearts. So B goes back to four Spades, and A, in his turn, discloses the Spades support, by going Six. There the bidding stops, and it will be seen that the six Spades can be made without any "fancy play," and even without a finesse being taken.

This hand is given as worthy of consideration, although it is clear that the six Spades bid might have been arrived at in other ways. For example, over A's bid of one Spade B might have shown Spade support first, going up to three to reveal not only Spade strength but strength outside. Then A might have shown the Ace of Diamonds clearly by a call of four Diamonds, while B, in his turn, could have called four Hearts, having no loser in that suit. These partners are really "looking" for the Ace of Clubs, and neither of them naming it or holding it, and each having one losing card in that suit, the Grand Slam is not bid.

A point that we should like to emphasize with reference to this bidding is that eventually the hand will be played in the strongest suit held by the two partners; the Heart bid is merely information, plainly telling all and sundry that there are no losing tricks in that suit. If B had also held the Ace of Clubs only, he could also have bid seven Clubs when A had bid the six Spades, and the seven Spades would then have been duly bid and made.

It may be suggested, by those not far advanced in

the Contract Bridge game, that this is all very complicated—the bidding, that is, when possibly four of a suit may be bid with a singleton Ace. "Asking for trouble!" is the way some people would describe it. Of course it would be asking for trouble if the partners did not each understand (and, also, each understand that the other fully understood) the principles on which bids are made; and, further, if it was not also understood that by "tricks" we mean "quick tricks."

There are other conventional bidding systems which are used by experienced players, but some are too complicated to give here. In any case the example of the "forcing two" (or "demand two") given is typical. Those who decide to play any of the conventions must make a special study of them, for they will not only have to agree with the player who happens to be a partner for a particular rubber as to the convention which is being played, but—as mentioned earlier—may also be requested to explain the convention to the opposition. The argument that the employment of conventions is tantamount to kicking the partner under the table or treading on his toes so many times is not a sound one, because the opponents know, as well as the partners, what the calls mean. At least, the opponents should know.

THE "INFORMATIVE DOUBLE." There is one simple convention in general use to which reference may be made—the "informative double." It is second player's turn to call, and the original caller has bid one in a suit. Second hand has some good cards—say three tricks—but no suit which he can safely overcall. Neither has he the suit which the original caller has bid. In such circumstances second caller's duty is to "double," his object being to tell his partner to declare his long suit; whereupon the partner must bid. It is an axiom of Contract that the double of one is never left in.

The partner bids in due course. Then how does the player who made the informative double know what his partner, who has been forced to bid, really holds? Elementary, my dear Watson! If the partner has a poor hand he makes the minimum response. But if he has a good hand he gives a "jump" bid—that is, calls three of his good suit instead of two.

It will be readily appreciated by those who have done no more than merely dabble in Contract that the scoring possibilities are great—much greater than in Auction. What looks like a bad rubber may be turned into quite a good one with a hand on which a Slam can be bid and made. A Grand Slam when Vulnerable, will turn a previous deficiency of 1,500 points into a balance of something more than 750 points.

Because the penalties for the players who go down—especially when Vulnerable—are so heavy, good players bear in mind the advantages of taking what might be called an "insurance policy" concerning a rubber. Three down doubled, when Vulnerable, means 900 points to the opposition, and as there is still an equal chance of winning the rubber after having put opponents down thus, it is better to take the nine hundred points—or possibly more—for the rubber, than run the risk of undertaking a game contract which is just beyond the making.

It is seldom wise to take a partner out of a business double unless, in the first place, there is an absolute certainty of making game or unless, in the second place, in the course of the bidding the partner who does thus take out has been guilty of telling his partner other than the truth. Those who have read these Contract notes thus far will not have been left in any doubt concerning the folly of telling a partner other than the truth concerning the hand.

"PSYCHIC" BIDS. The so-called "psychic" bids are all very well in their way, and nobody would go so far as to say that *in no circumstances* can they be justified, for this would be depriving the game of its element of chance, its opportunity, that is, of giving and taking risks. When the "psychic" bid comes off—when it stops the opposition, say, from going to rubber—the player responsible for it usually preens himself on his cleverness. As a matter of actual fact, however, it seldom happens that the "psychic" bid by one player does come off, unless his partner has some good trick-making cards which would have been useful against the opponents' bid in any case, Therefore, why bid " psychic ? "

While giving these hints on the bidding there is another point which experience suggests might usefully be made—a game cannot be scored at Contract unless a game is bid. We have seen that clearly enough. Hence the temptation, too strong to be resisted by many who play quite a lot, of taking a chance at going game; that is, bidding up to a game when there is no complete justification for believing that the game can be made on the cards held without a lot of unpredictable luck. Better to have two bites at the game cherry than two attempts to " force " a game out of a hand which does not justify the course. Two Hearts bid and made count 60 below the line, and the players who have the 60 below the line are in a good strategic position. Any subsequent two bid puts them to game, and when it is possible to make up a game score with a small bid the opposition will often be driven to more or less desperate measures to stop the game, and provide the opportunity for a fine business double—the " insurance policy " to which reference has been made.

Having pointed out the importance of walking warily, there is now the reverse side of the picture to be painted; viz., the question of deliberate sacrifice in order to prevent the opponents making the first game, or making the second game to give them rubber.

Obviously the first game has real value, and it may be considered worth while to sacrifice up to 450 points—that is three down—to prevent the opponents from winning it. Equally, as the rubber game—when opponents have no game to their credit—is worth almost as a minimum 800 points, a sacrifice here may also be considered worth while. Remembering, however, that the rubber game is worth 800 points, take the rubber when the opportunity arises, rather than give up the rubber merely to put 500 or 600 points to the score above the line by means of a double.

The scoring in Contract has been deliberately framed to penalize excessive flag-flying so severely that excessive flag-flying is not worth while. Hence anything in these notes which seems to advise, on occasion, the deliberate sacrifice of a few hundred points must be taken as it is meant to be given, i.e., with caution. The difficulty, clearly, with the calls which are made with the object of keeping the game alive, rather than with that of making the contract, is that the partner may take the calls too seriously. That is, he may think that the truth about the hand is being told when the fact is otherwise.

THE PLAY. There is little in the playing of the hands at Contract which is essentially different from the playing of the hands at Auction. The same general principles apply in regard to leads, finesses, etc., but there is one feature in Contract play which is worth bearing in mind. The calling, as already explained, is on what may be termed a very scientific basis, and after the calls at Contract have been duly made, the intelligent player should possess a fairly accurate mental picture of the hands that are still hidden from him. It is said that when four experts sit at the same table, they can, given accurate bidding, place practically every card in the four hands. Without trying to carry readers to that length, it is undoubtedly true that when players are bidding according to well-known conventions many cards can be placed with certainty, and the play of the hand by Declarer is naturally guided by the information conveyed by the correct use of the conventions. Take as an instance the original call of a suit meaning possibly three quick tricks in the caller's hand. When playing a hand after such a call, and looking at the other cards, the Declarer should be able to "place," say, the outside Ace.

In addition to the mental placing of the cards, there are certain lines of play (which apply to Auction as well as to Contract) to which reference may be made. "Covering an honour with an honour" is a formula well known, and is one which is all very well as a general principle; but the covering of an honour with an honour when there is a higher honour in third hand often has the effect of setting up a trick in the partner's hand. Whether or not, in any given case, the covering of an honour by an honour can serve any useful purpose, is a matter on which the discretion of the player must be exercised at the time.

Take a case in point from an actual hand recently seen. Hearts were trumps. A was the Declarer, and B his Dummy. The holdings of the four hands in Hearts were as follows:

"COVERING AN HONOUR WITH AN HONOUR"

It will be seen that there are five Hearts to be accounted for by the Declarer, with the Q as one of them. There may be three to the Queen in Z's hand. So A, trying to clear the Hearts and find the Q in passing, led the J of Hearts, through Y to Dummy's Ace. This was quite good play, for A was relying on the "cover an honour with an honour" formula; that is, relying on Y following that course. In playing in this way A accepted the opportunity of taking what is called the "switch finesse"—trying the J through and, if not covered, putting up the Ace in Dummy and then coming through Z with a finesse the other way.

The holder of Y hand could see from his hand what the game was. If he had put up the Q, thus covering the honour, no possible trick could come to the partners in the trump suit. So he played the 9 of Hearts on the J, refusing to cover. Thereupon A concluded that Q to three were likely to be held by Z, so up went the Ace from Dummy, the finesse against the Q was taken the other way, and of course Y made it—though it was all alone at the time.

FINESSING. There is a good general rule in regard to a finesse from which there should be no departure. Don't take a finesse unless you have to do so, even though it may seem fairly safe. An odd over-trick, or even two, in a straightforward call—in the absence, that is, of a double or redouble—doesn't make any real difference to the total number of points.

Experience teaches, however, that many players have a mistaken idea as to what really constitutes a finesse. A very common mistake, even among players who have played quite a lot, is to lead the Q through to an Ace in Dummy when neither the Declarer nor the Dummy had other big cards in the suit.

Suppose the holding of a suit, as between Declarer and his Dummy, is as here given :

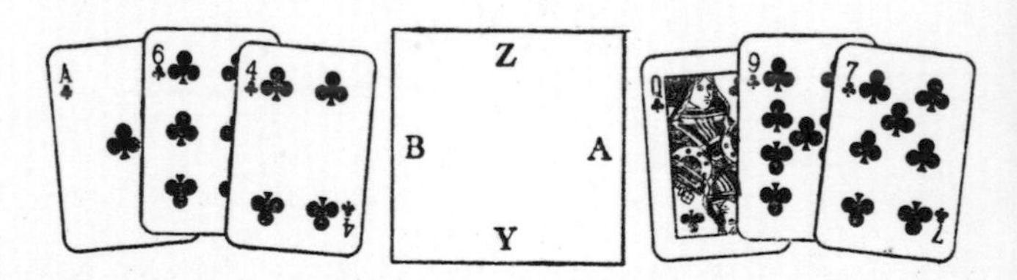

A COMMON MISTAKE IN FINESSING

Now the play of the Q by Declarer up to the Ace would be called by many players a finesse. Actually it should have a different title, for it comes under the heading of sheer foolishness. If the K is held by Y he will cover the Q, and then the J, 10 in the opponents' hands (they must be there as Declarer does not hold them) will be tricks.

With this holding there is only one real hope of making two tricks in the suit and that is to chance the K being on the right of Declarer. Therefore, the way to play this particular suit is—a small one from Dummy's hand up to the Declarer's.

Contract Bridge can now be left to the tender mercies of those who play it ; but as a last general observation, it should be definitely stated that the game is not nearly so fearsome as may appear on a first introduction. There is no necessity to be afraid of it, no necessity to be overwhelmed at the start by the bogey of complicated conventions. Just remember this ; if Aces and Kings are held at Contract, no power on earth can prevent them from making tricks. The little cards matter, but the big ones really count, and there is not the slightest necessity for headaches over systems.

WHIST

WHIST. Despite the understandable advance in popularity of some other card games, it is probably true to say that "ordinary" Whist is still actually played more than any other card game. Think of those Whist Drives which are such a popular form of raising money for this or that charity, of the family Whist played by the winter fire-side; and of the initiation into the mysteries of the game of those who are not yet old enough to begin to learn the intricacies of the so-called more "advanced" games.

Alas, it has to be said that hosts of people are content to play *at* Whist. "I don't play much, and I can't play very well," is a stock reply when an invitation to play Whist is given; but the giver of the invitation is by no means perturbed: "That doesn't matter, come along."

Actually, of course, this "ordinary" Whist is a very real game, demanding thought, card skill, concentration and team-work, if the full use is to be made of the cards. The satisfaction of having played a hand well—perhaps perfectly, of having "squeezed" a trick or two by a clever move—these are the things which make Whist (and other card games) worth while, and it is the intention of these notes so to explain the principles of correct play that the utmost use may be made of each hand.

RULES AND SCORING. Before proceeding to discuss the play in general, reference must be made to certain rules and regulations, and also to the recognised method of scoring—determining the winners—apart from the mere reckoning of the tricks won in each hand.

The rubber is the best of three games, and a game

consists of five points. The scoring of these points is as follows; each trick above six made in one hand counts one point, and the four honours (Ace, K, Q, J) are also included in the score towards game. If a player or his partner holds four honours in the trump suit they score four points, and for any three honours they score three points. Thus eight tricks to the two partners plus three honours count a game. One important feature of the honours scoring should, however, be noted; the players who, at the commencement of the deal, are at the score of four, cannot score honours.

The winners gain three points if their adversaries have not scored, two points when the opposition have scored not more than two points, and one point when their adversaries have scored more than two but not more than four. For the actual winning of the rubber two points are added to those already scored. It follows, of course, that in a rubber of three games the points gained by the losers in the one game they won, are deducted from the points gained by the winners in arriving at the total for settling purposes.

If at any time during the play a player fails to follow suit when he has one or more cards of the suit led, he is guilty of a REVOKE, the penalties for which are serious. The opponents of the player guilty of a revoke may take three tricks and add them to their own tricks, or deduct three points from the adversaries' score and add three to their own. The opponents of the revoking player may consult as to the penalty to be exacted.

The foregoing penalty may be claimed for as many revokes as take place during the hand, but it should be noted that the penalty cannot be divided; that is to say, the adversaries cannot add one or two to their own score, and deduct one or two from the side responsible for the revoke. One other point to note; in no circumstances can the revoking side score as the result of the hand in which the revoke occurred.

Four players make up a table. Having drawn for partners, and the partners having taken seats facing each other, the deal proceeds. The player cutting the lowest card has the right of first deal, and after due shuffling and a cut, he deals the cards one at a time, beginning with the player on his immediate left, and turning the last card (which of course falls to himself) face up, to determine trumps for that particular hand.

The official Laws of Whist contain many and minute directions laying down the procedure to be followed when mishaps (such as the exposure or touching of a card) occur during a deal. It is scarcely necessary for us to go deeply into such matters, but we should mention, in brief, that a card (other than the trump card) exposed during a deal necessitates a new deal by the same dealer. In order to lessen the chance of delay, annoyance, and possible penalties on such a score, the best rule to obey is—" all hands off the table "—until the deal is completed. Observation of that little point in the etiquette of the game saves a lot of trouble.

THE DEAL is not a proper one if the pack proves to be incorrect. If a card other than the last is exposed, a new deal is a sort of general order, but if it is agreed to carry on with the deal after a card has been exposed, then that card cannot be called at any time during the play.

In some circles the trump suit is decided by a cut from another pack, with the card turned up exposed throughout the playing of the hand; but according to the strict rules of the game the last card should be turned up to determine trumps. That card remains exposed until the dealer has played to the first trick, then he gathers it up and places it with his other cards.

The deal being properly completed, the player on the left of the dealer has the first lead. Thereafter each member of the party follows in turn until all four have played, the player of the highest card in the suit led taking the trick unless it is trumped.

PLAY OF THE HAND. During the play of the hand it sometimes happens that a player accidentally exposes a card other than the one he actually means to play. Any card so exposed is liable to be called by the opponents at such time as they deem fit, but a card called in this way must not be played if, by so doing, the player is compelled to revoke.

If a player leads out of turn, i.e. when he has not won the previous trick, his opponents may call the card led in error, or may demand the lead of a particular suit when it is the next turn of either "guilty" player or his partner to lead.

Now for the play itself. In the first place it is very necessary for each one of the four players to make up his mind, from the moment the first card is led, that he will watch every card as it falls—"count the pips"—as the popular wording has it. There is, or should be, significance in every card put on the table, and the smaller members of a suit may become of extreme importance during the play of the later tricks in the hand.

The next point to stress is that Whist is essentially a partnership game. The player who considers his own hand, ignoring the "calls," the signals and the requirements of his partner, can never be a good player. Remembering the great importance of successful co-operation, one object of each lead, of each card played, should be to give reliable information to the partner, in as clear a manner as possible. There can be very effective talk between partners without a word being said, and the "conversations" are quite in order, because the opponents are "listening in." In other words there are generally accepted conventions in this game of Whist; they are not at all complicated, but it is very necessary that they should be learnt and borne in mind in order that the hand may be properly played. Take, for instance, the opening lead. There is unanimity among the experts to the effect that a player, in ordinary circumstances, makes the lead of the suit which he wants returned if and when his partner is "in."

It may be argued against such "conventional leads" that though they do give information to one partner they, at the same time, give it to two opponents. That is true, but it can't be helped; and experience shows very plainly that, within certain limits, knowledge conveyed is more valuable to the partner than to the opposition; at all events this knowledge is selected.

OPENING LEADS. Now we may consider some opening leads. In this connection it is helpful to contemplate the varied hands from which the leader will be called upon to make his selection for the first lead. The hand may be a bad one; but even so there must be discretion in the lead. If, for instance, it contains no strong suit and four comparatively small cards of a suit other than trumps, the fourth best of this longest suit is the safe lead. It tells the partner where at least four cards of that suit are held; and, looking at the lead in conjunction with his own hand, the partner may be able to determine fairly accurately the value of the cards held by the player making the opening lead.

When big cards of a suit of fair length are held by the original leader his task is comparatively simple. The immediate, or ultimate, object of almost any lead is to make tricks in the suit led.

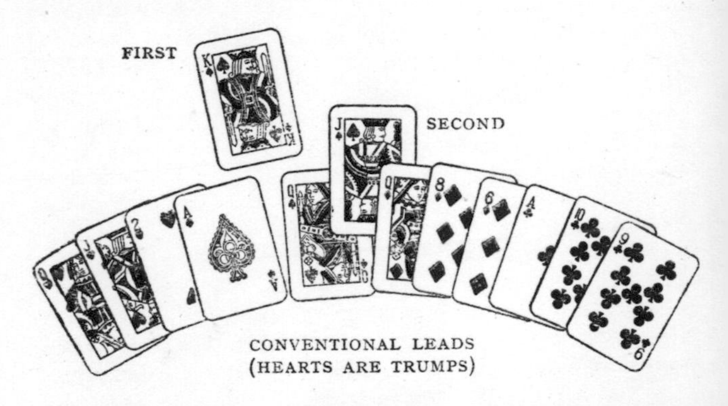

CONVENTIONAL LEADS
(HEARTS ARE TRUMPS)

On the next page is a list of what may be called conventional leads from given cards, and a study of the Table will show the manner in which the player making the lead is "talking" information to his partner.

Table of Original and Second Leads

When Holding, in Non-Trump Suits	First	Second
A, K, Q, J *(see diagram,* p. 52)	K	J
A, K, Q	K	Q
A, K and others	K	A
A, K only	A	K
K, Q, J with one small ...	K	J
K, Q, J with others	J	K, if five; Q, if more
A and several small	A	4th best of small ones
K, Q and others	K	If K makes, 4th best
A, Q, J alone, or with one small	A	Q
A, Q, J with two or more ...	A	J
K, J, 10, 9	9	K, if A or Q is played on first round.
K, J, 10	10	
Q, J, 10, 9	Q	9
Q, J and one small	Q	
Q, J and others	4th best	

When Holding, in Trump Suit	First	Second
A, K, Q, J	J	Q
A, K, Q	Q	K
A, K, and five others	K	A
A, K and four (or less) small ...	4th best	

Consider, for a moment, what some of these leads convey. If Ace, K, and small cards of a suit (other than the trump suit) are held, the lead of the K will tell the partner two things. First that Ace is held as well as the K, and that there are at least two others—possibly three—of the same suit in the hand. It will be noted that in some instances in the Table the K is led before the Ace to show that the holder has the latter and some others. In the event, however, of Ace and K of a suit being held "bare," the Ace and then the K are led as an indication that these are all the cards held by the leader in that suit. This "Ace, K only" suit is not advised for an opening lead, however; such cards can usually be better employed later.

The establishment of a long suit (the best suit) is a desirable end. Here is a typical example of a hand on which an attempt should be made to establish the long suit—Hearts. Spades are trumps, A is the original leader:

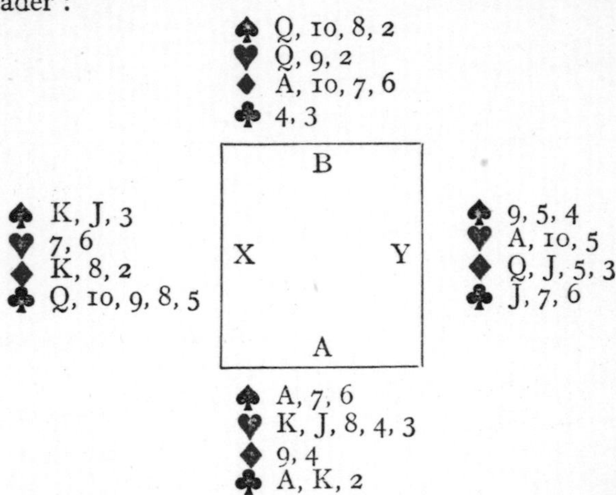

The lead made by A, carrying out the principle of the fourth highest of the longest suit, is 4 of Hearts; on this X plays low; B, the partner of A, plays the Q, drawing Y's Ace, with the result that when the suit is next led, it is established. Hence, when trumps are finished A's Hearts will be trick makers, for he is sure to be "in" later in the hand with his winning cards of other suits. A display of the fact that Ace and K of Clubs are held would not be good play for the original leader from this hand; he will need both later on.

It is not suggested that there should never be any departure from the leads as given in the Table, but when the holding is such that a lead of a safe type can be made, experience proves that as a rule it should be made.

There is one opening lead which still appeals so strongly to the imagination of certain players that they are unable to resist the temptation to try it. This is the lead of a singleton, i.e., the only card held, of a plain (non-trump) suit. Unfortunately, it is one of those leads which, if it comes off, is reckoned very clever, for it enables the leader to make one or perhaps two small trumps which would otherwise have been valueless. Experience proves, however, that this temptation should be resisted. Shortness of a suit in one hand must inevitably mean length of that same suit in one of the other three hands, and as two of them belong to the opposition, it follows that the odds are that length in that suit will be held by one or other of the opponents. After all, and speaking generally, there is no need for this desperate hurry to "ruff," or trump, a suit of which only a singleton is held; it is sure to be led by one of the players in due course.

Suppose, however, that the coup comes off at the first trick—that the partner of the player making the lead of a singleton takes it with the Ace and returns the suit, thus enabling the original leader to make a small trump. There still remains, for the original leader, the question of how to get his partner in again. The opponents will quickly sense any effort he may make to do so, and will soon queer his pitch if they possibly can. Having stopped the attempt, and being put wise as to the singleton, the probability is that trumps will be led.

SECOND PLAYER. Following naturally upon the original lead, there is now to be considered the play of the other members of the party. Connected with this game of Whist, as with other games, certain slogans have passed into currency and are in continual use. But just as one is not expected invariably and at all times to act on slogans in other fields (to "Eat more

Fish," for instance, when one is thoroughly tired of it), so with the slogans at Whist—they are by no means immutable, nor of pontifical weight and authority *in every case.* Indeed a very little thought will show that the possible combinations of the cards are so numerous and the situations of the game so various that there is no room for words such as "never" or "always" in the vocabulary of any game at cards.

One of the Whist slogans which has persisted through the ages is "Second player plays low"; and very good too, for ordinary occasions, for it has commonsense behind it. With the second player playing low, third must go high, and the fourth player is then provided with the opportunity of taking a high card from his opponent's hand with a still higher one. There are circumstances, however, in which this would be bad advice to follow; e.g., suppose the lead is the fourth card of what is clearly not a very strong suit, and second hand holds the big cards of that suit—K, Q, J and another. The risk of second playing his small card is too great in this case, and he should put down the lowest of his high sequence, thus giving information to his partner and eliminating the possibility of third hand winning the trick with a small card.

Second player may also have the sort of hand with which it is desirable to get in quickly so as to give his own partner some idea of the "lie of the land." Thus we see that "Second player low" is merely one of those instructions which, like some other rules, must be disregarded from time to time, according to circumstances and the make-up of the particular hand.

THIRD PLAYER. Passing round the table to third player there is another slogan which is applied (or misapplied, as the case may be), viz., "Third player plays high," if the lead from his partner is a low one in the suit. This is a convention arising from "Second player low," but it must not be taken that it is always wise for third to play the highest of the suit led. Suppose, for instance, that he holds Ace, Q of the suit of which his partner has led his small fourth best. It follows that if the K is held by fourth player it must make. There is a possibility (an even chance) that the K is held by second player. In any case the only way to get tricks with both Ace and Q in such circumstances is for third player to play the Queen.

The finesse against one's partner, as such play is often wrongly described, must be used with discretion. If it is clear from the original lead that both partners have length in the same suit, then the finesse may prove tragic, as there remains the possibility of fourth hand having K only, making it, and in due course proceeding to trump the other high cards of that suit.

There is another consideration which enters into the play of third hand; care must be taken not to block what is clearly one's partner's long suit. If third hand has only Ace, Q of the suit originally led, and it is decided to finesse the Q—if this wins the trick the Ace should be returned immediately, thus unblocking the suit, and making it possible to convey to the partner by the lead of another suit the clear information that no others are held in the original suit.

Care must be exercised in other ways, too, not to block the partner's suit. Consider the lead of Ace of a non-trump suit, thus conveying the information that five of that suit are in the leading hand. Now the partner may hold K, Q, J and a small one. In such circumstances use of the small one on the original lead would eventually block the suit; so the proper play is the J on the first lead and Q on the second, even though a trump should intervene, the small card being retained for the purpose of putting the partner in again later. Here and there will be found, at the end of a hand, that the unblocking may have cost a trick, but the principle of unblocking laid down is undoubtedly sound.

Among the first general principles for third hand that has taken the trick in the suit originally led, is the return not merely of that suit, but of the highest card held in it. But even this, like the other good general precepts, must be often disregarded for the purposes of an immediate return lead. The player may have something in his hand which he wants to show his partner, and he should take this (the first) opportunity of giving information. Having given his information (having shown a strong suit) third player will not, however, during the play of the hand, forget the suit which his partner originally led.

When a partner asks for a suit give it to him ; then, if for some reason or other, he did not really want it, it is not the funeral of the third player. In the event of recriminations at the end of the hand, he can always retort, "Why did you ask for the suit if you did not want it ?" That should silence criticism—and complaint !

There is no real necessity to discuss the play of fourth hand ; all he has to do is to take the trick if he can.

As the play of the hand progresses, so will the situation of the remaining cards be revealed, more or less accurately, to the players who are watching the fall of the cards. Subsequent play must be framed accordingly.

TRUMPS. One of the biggest problems which faces Whist players (no matter what their position at the table) is, when to lead trumps. Reluctance to lead the trump suit is a weakness of many Whist players, and everybody must have heard the oft-repeated regrets for the people who are sleeping on the Embankment because they would not lead trumps, fondly imagining that such cards have more value lying "doggo" in their hand than when playing their part in the battle. It still remains true, that among the occasional (as distinct from the regular) players of the game, the lead of a trump originally (or at any early stage in the hand) will often bring an involuntary cry from the partner : "Do you know those are trumps ?" All wrong, of course, but a fact !

Logically, this reluctance to lead trumps is unsound in many cases. If there is a good hand apart from trumps, and an ordinary holding in trumps, the advantages of leading the latter are obvious. By carrying on with the good strong suits, and leaving the trumps alone, the risk is run of having the good hand "torn to ribbons" by trumps from the opposing hands.

"It was bad luck having the Ace of Clubs trumped, wasn't it, partner?" is a remark often heard. Quite frequently the correct retort would be—"Not at all! It wasn't bad luck, it was *bad play!*"

The possession of a strong hand of trumps should be used for the purpose of drawing the trumps of the opposition. There cannot be any doubt concerning this as a general principle. With five or more it is good play to start with a trump lead. Never mind about the other cards; they won't make any tricks if they are small ones without length, and the partner may have a good strong suit which will "stand up" when the trumps have been extracted from the hands of the opponents.

One of the intricate matters on which questions are often put by those who have not fully mastered the game, concerns the advisability of "ruffing" when unable to follow suit. Taking into consideration the possibility of the partner being able to win the trick, *should a trump be used on this doubtful suit?*

The general answer is "Yes," if the player has only two or three small trumps which cannot possibly be of service when trumps are led in due course. If fair strength in trumps is held, it may be considered desirable to hold those trumps, especially if there are other strong cards, or a suit which has been established, in the hand. In such cases it may even be good policy to allow a master card to pass untrumped, if there is no risk of losing the game in consequence. If, however, the masters of a suit are led more than once, showing the opponents to be strong in that suit, then a trump will have to be sacrificed.

It is fairly safe to assume that a player can afford to trump in (even in a doubtful case) if he has more than four trumps. The possession of trumps up to six in number will justify a player in trumping any trick about which he is not certain, and in leading the trumps forthwith. Much the same principle applies to the over-trumping of an opponent. With four trumps in hand, and a suit already established, it may be advisable to allow the adversary to take the trick. He has then one trump fewer, and one's own fourth trump may eventually be very useful in securing the lead so that the tricks of the established suit may then be made.

Incidentally, this readiness or otherwise to trump should convey a lot to an intelligent partner. The player who does not trump when he can do so conveys to his partner, or should be doing so, that he has fair strength in trumps, and some good cards still concealed. The readiness to trump suggests either very real length in trumps, or the possession of trump cards which would be useless if trumps were led.

DISCARDING—that is, the throwing away of cards when a player is void of the suit led—must be done upon some sort of system. It is generally agreed that in ordinary circumstances, the lowest card of a weak suit should be discarded, but from time to time the situation will be such that the discard should be a high one. To give an extreme case ; suppose, after several tricks have gone, Clubs have not been played. Of this suit, the player on whom rests the onus of discarding holds all the master cards. With a view to " compelling " his partner to lead Clubs if and when he gets in, the Ace of that suit can safely be discarded.

From the desperate haste shown by some players to make tricks one might imagine that Aces and Kings have a habit of flying out of the window ! Remember that if the opponents lead a suit the idea behind the lead is probably the establishment of that suit. If one or two high cards in it are held, there is no point in playing them, i.e., in returning the lead of the opponents. Keep command of the suit led by them if possible.

TENACE. In the later stages of the hand, when the situation of most of the remaining cards is known, the odd trick can often be snatched by the process of " throwing the lead " up to what is called a tenace, i.e., the best and third best remaining cards of a suit.

Here is an end-game which shows how this can be done, Spades are trumps and Y has the lead :

Y, having taken the previous trick, has now to lead, either from his K of Spades or Ace of Hearts. If he leads from his K of Spades he cannot make a trick in that

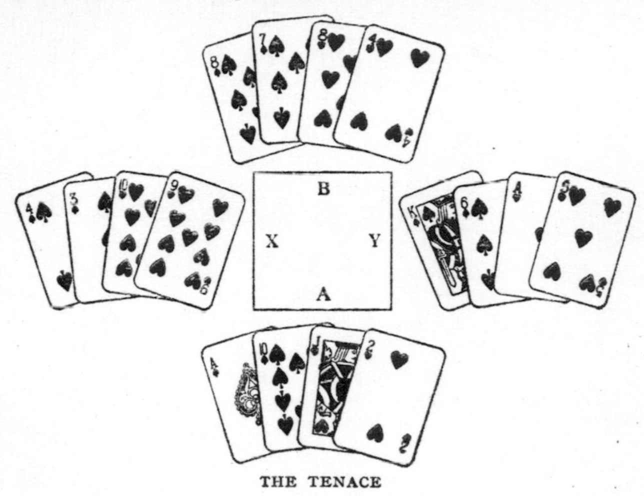

THE TENACE

suit. So he leads the Ace of Hearts on which A must throw the J, as he does not want to be compelled to lead from his tenace in trumps, as he would have to do after taking the next trick if he now threw the 2. A having thrown his big Heart, it does not matter whether X or B can take the next Heart trick—the lead must be up to the ace-ten of Spades in A's hand and he must make both tricks.

SOLO WHIST

Solo Whist may justifiably be described as the best of the "whole-pack" games for occasional play by a party of four. It calls for much skill and the possession of at least the average amount of card sense, and it has certain advantages over whist and the bridge games. One such advantage is that each hand is complete in itself. Thus the play can cease at any moment when the players so desire, and there is no counting up of points—though the indifferent player may have to count up the cost!

Another reason, as will be shown later, why Solo Whist appeals is that there is a considerable amount of variety in the play. The partners are changing continually, and from time to time it is a case of three players against one. There is the possibility, too, of a really bad hand proving a very good one, from the point of view of interest.

Incidentally, Solo Whist is also a game for a little gamble at any stakes convenient to the pockets of the players; indeed, many will maintain that it is literally true that the game cannot be properly played or enjoyed without some stake being attached to it. Our mental make-up is such that, in the absence of something tangible to "go for," players will take all sorts of unjustifiable risks, and the play, in consequence, may become little more than farcical.

Four players complete an ordinary Solo Whist table, but there is no reason why a fifth player, if available, should not take his part in the game. In such cases the fifth player—usually the one immediately behind the deal—stays out of one hand in every five, but the custom is for him to pay or receive, according as the call is made or goes down, on single calls.

The party duly assembled, the player with the lowest card cut has the cards properly "made" and then deals in a way different from that common to most games—viz., three cards at a time to each player in turn until the last round; then one to each player, the last card being turned face up in front of the dealer to determine the trump suit for that particular hand.

THE "CALLING"—that is to say the making of statements as to what it is hoped to do with the particular hand—starts with the player on the left of the dealer. Here it is necessary to enumerate the calls, and they are given in their proper order—that is from the lowest upwards—

Pass	Abondance
Proposal	Abondance in Trumps
Acceptance	Misère Ouverte
Solo	Abondance Déclarée
Misère	

Certain points concerning the calls should be noted. In the case of a *pass*, the second player (or the third or fourth in due course) have the same options open to them, provided there have been no intermediate calls. When there is a *proposal*, there can be an *acceptance* from any subsequent player—in the absence of higher calls. It should also be noted that in the case of an unaccepted proposal from a player other than the one who had the first call, the original caller *(but the original caller only)* has the option of accepting.

Nothing in the shape of previous calls prevents a subsequent player from making a higher call. There may be a *solo* or any other higher call over a *proposal*; even a solo over a proposal which has been accepted, and so on right through the calls. This proviso should be borne in mind—that a player who has passed cannot take further part in the calling, unless he is "fifth" player, as explained in the previous paragraph.

A player who has called with other than a proposal can revise his call to any of greater value than the call which has intervened. For example, suppose third player calls *misère*, fourth player may then go *abondance*. The caller of misère, in his due turn, may call *misère ouverte*, while, also in his turn, the abondance caller is then left free to call *abondance déclarée* if he so desires.

To put this apparently complicated matter in simple form : the players who have already begun to compete in the calling may continue to compete, if they feel disposed to do so, in turn, but the competition for the call must only be on the overcall system.

We will now explain the meaning of the various calls, beginning, as before, with the lowest.

A PROPOSAL means that the caller contracts to make in partnership with any one member of the table who accepts the proposal eight tricks, playing the hand with the trump suit as originally turned up by the dealer. Here note that if the first caller has proposed and has not been accepted, he may revise his call to SOLO, but he is under no obligation to do so. It should also be noted, in passing, that when a proposal has been made and accepted, the players retain their original places at the table. Thus first and second players behind the deal may be playing "prop" and "cop" hands as partners.

A call of SOLO is an undertaking on the part of one player to make five tricks himself, playing against the other three players, with the trump suit as exposed.

The caller of MISÈRE declares that he has a hand which he hopes, in spite of the efforts of the three opponents, will not take a single trick. In this call there is no trump suit.

A call of ABONDANCE implies the making of at least nine tricks with the one hand, the declarer announcing the trump suit for that particular hand when the calling is finished, but not previously. That is important. If the call is ABONDANCE IN TRUMPS, which exceeds an ordinary abondance call, the declarer undertakes to make nine tricks with the trumps as originally determined.

On a MISÈRE OUVERTE call the caller declares that he will not take a trick despite the fact that his cards—but not those of the other players—are exposed on the table for all to see after the first trick has been played.

ABONDANCE DÉCLARÉE is an undertaking to make all the thirteen tricks with the one hand, the declarer having the advantage of deciding the trump suit. In this case *only*, the caller has the first lead. In all other calls the first lead is made by the player on the immediate left of the dealer. Thereafter the lead is from the hand which took the previous trick.

STAKES. As the question of tricks under or over the call is clearly important, the stake ratio usually adopted may be interposed here. The agreed stakes may be of any dimensions, of course, but the calls have different values and the ratio between them must be maintained whatever the basic stake—pounds, shillings, or pence—counters or nuts. Suppose, for instance, it is agreed to play on what is called the " three, six, nine, twelve " stake principle; this would mean that (1) a *proposal* and *acceptance*, duly made, would result in one opponent paying three points to one other opponent; (2) a *solo* call made would bring a six-points stake to the caller from each of the three opponents; (3) a *misère* call nine points from each of them, and (4) *abondance* twelve points. The foregoing makes no provision for the *misère ouverte* calls, or for *abondance déclarée*. The usual mode of procedure with these is to double the ordinary calls of the same nature, viz., payment would be eighteen points for *misère ouverte*, and twenty-four for *abondance déclarée*.

Overtricks—and undertricks—are paid for in single units, but in the case of *misère, misère ouverte* and *abondance déclarée* the actual stake only is considered; that is, no question of overtricks or undertricks enter into these calls. If all the players *pass*, or there is no acceptance of a proposal, the cards are thrown in for the next deal. In this connection it is usual to establish a pool or " kitty," into which each player pays an agreed amount (doubled after a hand has been thrown in) at each deal; this goes to the next player duly fulfilling a contract on a single call. In some schools it is the rule that a player failing to make a single call has to pay into the " kitty " a sum equal to the amount that it happens to contain at the moment.

RULES OF SOLO WHIST. Certain cardinal rules of Solo Whist may conveniently be mentioned here.

The dealer leaves the turned-up card on the table until he has played to the first trick. Thereafter it is permissible for any player at the table to enquire, and to be told, what is the trump suit, but not the value of the card turned up.

If a player *proposes* before his turn, he must withdraw the call. If, afterwards, there is a proposal, the player who has proposed out of turn cannot accept, though the out of turn proposal does not prevent him from making an overcall such as solo.

If a player should call *solo* out of turn, and a player in front of him calls *misère,* then the caller of *misère* may demand a lead of the original trump suit at the first lead, but not later in the hand. This same rule applies in the case of a call of *abondance in trumps* out of turn, if there is a *misère ouverte* call from a player who should have had the earlier call.

The reason for this "call of a trump lead" in such circumstances should be explained. By a call of *solo,* or *abondance in trumps,* the other players are presumed to know the situation of the strong cards in the trump suit, and the caller of *misère* might be handicapped by the possession of such knowledge by his opponents.

It often happens that a proposal is made and a succeeding player, not having heard the proposal, also proposes. The second player cannot then amend his call to an acceptance if there is objection raised to such course, but he retains the right to make a higher call.

In the case of a card exposed by a player not trying to "make" an individual call, such card must be left face upwards on the table, and may be called at the bidder's discretion. A card exposed by a player after he has played to a particular trick cannot be called on that trick, but may be called later.

A player revoking—not following to the suit led when he has a card or cards of that suit—forfeits three tricks for every revoke, and these are added to the opponents' tricks. This three trick penalty is exacted from the gross tricks of the revoking player or players. For example: if the proposer and accepter make eleven tricks in a hand in which either of them has revoked, the deduction of the three tricks would leave them with eight. They would then not have to pay under-tricks penalties, but would, of course, have to pay the penalty for going down, as they cannot win a hand on a revoke. Should the two players make only nine tricks in all, however, after a revoke, they would then pay on two under-tricks. If both sides revoke in the same hand there can be no win or loss, merely a new deal.

Certain rules of the game are applicable only to the hands in which *misère* is being played. In playing this call no player is permitted to see a trick after it has been turned and quitted. If any player, other than the caller, leads or plays to a trick out of turn, exposes a card, or revokes, the caller can claim to have made good his *misère* contract, and the offending player pays all the stakes. When the *misère* call has been defeated, the other three players must expose all their remaining cards so that the caller may have the opportunity of noting whether a revoke has occurred.

It has already been mentioned that the gambling element—that is, the opportunity for taking a risk—is among the appeals which Solo Whist makes. There is just one general hint which should be given. In playing this game always bear in mind that the cards have been dealt three at a time. Consequently the chances are that the distribution of the suits in the various hands will be much less even than they usually are at the games in which the cards are dealt one at a time. Many calls are certainties; others have in them the element of chance, and thus entail the necessity of reckoning the odds.

We can now consider the calls, and give some general hints on playing to them.

The first player behind the deal (i.e., to the left of the dealer) has the first call, and in relation to his calls there is an important consideration with which the other players are not concerned, viz., his chance of having a second call. It is for this reason that a hand which would justify a *proposal* from a second player is, as a general thing, no more than a *pass* from the point of view of first caller.

As a principle generally accepted—though not invariably—it is assumed by the other players that the player making the proposal is fairly strong in the trump suit. A fair holding of trumps (even, say, five to the Queen) would be a good proposal provided other honour cards were held in the hand. To put it in another way, the proposal should come from the player who has not fewer than four certain tricks in his own hand, with a possibility of making five when assisted by a partner.

Assuming that the proposer has a fairly good hand of trumps he can be accepted by a subsequent caller who, though not strong in trumps, possesses trick-making cards in the plain suits. Then they can go ahead—in the absence of an over-call—to make their eight tricks. The fact that either the proposer or the accepter (the "Prop" and the "Cop," as they are called) probably has strength in the trumps—generally the proposer—leads us to a definite conclusion concerning the playing of the hand; that as a general rule trumps can be led. Woe usually befalls the partners in a proposal and acceptance game when neither feels in a position to lead trumps.

A player when accepting of course takes into consideration the fact that he is going into partnership with one who has already declared a certain amount of strength; consequently he realizes that cards in his own hand which could not be counted as winners by themselves, have quite a good chance of taking a trick when functioning as part of a combine. For example, Kings, when held by a player playing an individual call, have scarcely any value at all; but when held by a player who is accepting a proposal Kings may be considered to constitute possible tricks. Three tricks and a "bit"—that is, a possible fourth trick if the hand does well—would be quite enough to allow one to accept a proposal.

The lead of trumps at an early stage of a joint call is merely carrying out the idea which is applied to ordinary whist—leading the long suit. One or other of the callers must have fair strength and length in the trump suit.

The objective in leading them is to deprive the opponents of their trumps.

Occasionally it is suspected—or discovered—that both the proposer and accepter were strong in trumps, and not too strong in the non-trump suits. They will then try the "ruffing" method of making eight tricks, and the opponents in turn, will lead trumps to defeat this plan of campaign.

Here are typical hands for a "proposal" and "acceptance" call of what might be called the strong type:

SPADES Trumps: The King is exposed. First and Second Pass.

Third Proposes on:

SPADES—ACE, 7, 4, 2; CLUBS—Q, J, 5; DIAMONDS—K, 6; HEARTS—ACE, K, 6, 4

Fourth Accepts on:

SPADES—K, 10, 8, 3; CLUBS—ACE, K, 8, 4; DIAMONDS—ACE, HEARTS—Q, J, 10, 3

The Solo Call—the making of five tricks, with trumps determined by the exposed card—does not present any big difficulty. The tricks should be comparatively easy to reckon. Trumps, generally speaking, are the backbone of a Solo Call, but this is not an invariable rule.

The "snag" of the call is the expectancy, still retained by many players, of making tricks because the master cards of a long suit are held. This optimism is seldom justified. Ace, K, and one other of a suit may rightly be regarded as two tricks; but Ace, K, to six of a non-trump suit cannot really be relied upon for even one trick in a Solo Call.

Many a Solo Call has been bid and made on Ace, K, Ace, K, Ace—the necessary five tricks—of three comparatively short suits, with nothing else of value in the hand, but such calls have an element of risk. There is another consideration which, quite justifiably, may influence a player in making a solo declaration; i.e. his holding in trumps, plus the fact that the player on his right has already proposed. On the assumption that the proposer has some good trumps, the trump cards in the solo caller's hand appear to have additional value. For example, the A, Q, of trumps may, with fair confidence, be reckoned as two tricks if there has been a proposal from the player on the right—and so on. Better a safe acceptance than a risky solo is a good principle to work upon.

Consider a player holding a hand such as the following, in which there is a real temptation to call *Solo :*

SPADES—8, 4, 3; CLUBS—ACE, K;
DIAMONDS—ACE, 10, 7, 6, 4, 2; HEARTS—ACE, Q

In the endeavour to make five tricks with such a hand, a solo caller would probably not make more than three. The lead against him would most likely be in Diamonds. This would be taken with the Ace. The A, K of Clubs might then be led by the caller, or possibly a trump in the hope of getting a lead to the A, Q of Hearts; but the minute the caller lost the lead Diamonds would come back, he would have to follow, and one or other of his opponents would be getting rid of losers in the Heart suit—which would be trumped in due course.

The next higher call over solo is *misère*—the undertaking to play the hand right through without the caller making a single trick. It has been said—with more than a germ of truth—that the *misère* call is the short cut to the workhouse. What may appear on the face of it a perfectly good hand for the purpose can, by skilful play on the part of the three opponents, be made to win a trick. The long suit without the deuce—how many times has *misère* caller been compelled to pay as the result of such holding! The possession of a single card in one suit—not too high—and a risky card in another suit is the sort of hand on which a chance is often taken, but it frequently comes "unstuck." The hope of a risky card being discarded on the singleton suit is seldom realized, for there are very real reasons why the short suit will not be led by the players playing against the *misère* call.

Another point to be borne in mind is respect of a risky *misère*, is the place whence the first lead will come. It may be the *misère* caller's own lead, which is a disadvantage, as he will then have to advertise to his opponents the suit in which he is, apparently, invincible. And they, in due course, will proceed to try the other suits. A bad place for the lead to a *misère* is on the immediate right of the caller, as a comparatively small card will be led through and third and fourth players can dispense with the high cards in that suit.

The real interest in the *misère* call, once it has been made, is the play against the call, and it is safe to say that this provides the biggest problem in solo whist play. Playing against *misère* is not easy. Lead from the short suit, not the long one, is a good general principle, because the leader's short suit is most likely to be the caller's long one. Here is a typical hand, showing all the cards.

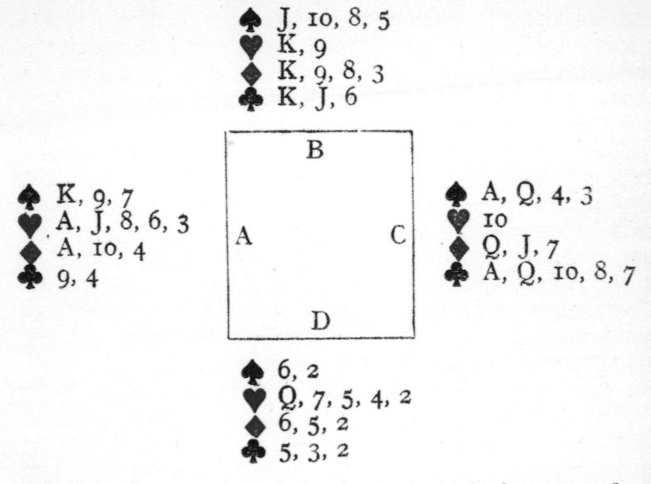

This is a hand on which D, the dealer, who has turned up the four of Hearts as trump-card, may venture *misère*, and it looks a good hand. Consider first a point in calling, and then the play as it is likely to go. A, the first caller, proposed, suggesting—as previously explained—strength in trumps. B has possibly passed, C has accepted, showing strength outside trumps, and D chances *misère*.

It is A's lead, and he is not in the best position, but he follows a good plan in leading from his short suit—the 9 of Clubs would be quite a good lead. On this B would probably go up, and C still higher with the Ace of Clubs, thus taking the trick. The length of the Clubs in C's hand—and the strength of them—make the suit a bad one to return, so C leaves it and leads his single ten of Hearts. This is the lead which, as will be seen, can eventually put D down. D plays the seven, A the Ace, B the King. A should now sense that D has the Queen of Hearts, and can quickly discover, by leading back the suit, that B has only the nine and C has none at all. So the continuance of this suit will eventually cause D to take a trick with the Queen.

The call of *abondance* is quite simple, for the player

making the call should be able to reckon up his nine tricks—making his own trumps—provided there is anything save a really freak distribution in any one of the other three hands. Freak distributions, however, have a knack of happening far too often!

One point is self-evident: that the caller of *abondance* must hold plenty of trumps. A two-suit hand—such as A, K, Q, to six trumps, and A, K, Q, to five of an outside suit looks absolutely safe. That is, indeed, the sort of hand on which *abondance* may be called. But it by no means follows that it will make the nine tricks. There may be five trumps to the J, 10, ranged in one hand against the caller, and the distribution of the caller's weak suits will be such that, almost inevitably, the opponents will lead the suit which he will have to "ruff." Indeed, this is the ideal way for opponents to play against the *abondance* caller: to make him trump and keep on trumping, thus weakening the hand and compelling him to lead.

Everything which has been said in reference to calls of *abondance* applies when *abondance in trumps* is undertaken. The *misère ouverte*, and the *abondance déclarée* should not be called unless they are, practically speaking, "certs." In the *misère ouverte*, any suit which has three or four cards in it without the deuce is almost certain to lead to downfall. The fact that there is no deuce will be spotted after the first lead; the opposition will play suits on which all the opponents can throw away, and the deuce will be led in due course.

AUCTION SOLO

A variation of Solo Whist, known as Auction Solo, may be mentioned. The title explains the game; it is an auction. Proposals and Acceptances are, as a rule, cut out of this game, and practically all that is necessary to mention is the calls in order, starting from the lowest:

Solo of 5 tricks.
Solo of 5 tricks in trump suit.
Solo of 6 tricks.

Solo of 6 tricks in trump suit.
Solo of 7 tricks.
Solo of 7 tricks in trump suit.
Solo of 8 tricks.
Solo of 8 tricks in trump suit.
Misère.
Abondance of 9 tricks.
Abondance of 9 tricks in trump suit.
Abondance of 10 tricks.
Abondance of 10 tricks in trump suit.
Abondance of 11 tricks.
Abondance of 11 tricks in trump suit.
Abondance of 12 tricks.
Abondance of 12 tricks in trump suit.
Misère Ouverte.
Abondance déclarée with no trumps.
Abondance déclarée in trump suit.

One point about Auction Solo which is really important is that during the auction the caller does not name the suit—unless it is the original trump suit—until the calling is finished.

PIQUET

PIQUET is perhaps the best game for two, as it is, apparently, the simplest; but short acquaintance will show that foresight and judgement are required if the best is to be made of the cards. It appears to have originated in Italy and, as is evidenced by its special terms, reached England through France. A book on it—translated from the French—appeared as early as 1657, but it was not until 1882, when RUBICON PIQUET superseded the earlier form *Piquet au Cent*, and became the standard game, that the Code of Laws now in force was promulgated by the Portland and Turf Clubs.

This standard game is played with one pack from which all the cards below 7 have been taken, the remaining thirty-two cards ranking from Ace to 7. There are no trumps. In cutting, the Ace counts high, and the player cutting the higher card has choice of seats and first deal.

Either player may shuffle, the dealer, or "Younger Hand" having the right both of shuffling last and of the cut; he deals out twelve cards to each alternately, two or three at a time, placing the eight remaining cards (known as the *Stock* or *Talon*) face downwards at his side, either in one packet or with the top five lying across the bottom three, for the five belong to the Elder Hand (the non-dealer) and the three to the dealer. The stock plays a very important part in the game, as will be seen later.

The object of the players is to score as many points as possible for the value of certain combinations held, and to win tricks in the subsequent play. Scores are kept on a score-sheet or may be marked on a cribbage board. The scoring combinations, and the order in which they have to be called, are as follows; the players call them and if they are admitted to be "good," score for them at once.

CARTE BLANCHE is a hand devoid of K, Q or J; it

scores ten points. Carte Blanche is shown by displaying the cards, face upwards, on the table. As soon as either player finds that he has Carte Blanche he must so inform his opponent, but Dealer need not show his cards until his opponent has discarded.

POINT is a suit of cards, not necessarily in sequence. The player having the longer suit scores one for each of its component cards; e.g., a Point of Five, if good, counts five, a Point of Six, six, and so on. If, as frequently happens, both players have Points of the same length the pip-value is taken (Aces being reckoned as 11, court cards as 10, and the lower cards at their face value), and the more valuable Point is the only one that scores; if the players still tie neither scores for Point.

SEQUENCE is a series of three or more cards of the same suit in order, such as Ace, K, Q, J; J, 10, 9, etc.; Sequences are known as *Tierce* (3), *Quart* (4), *Quint* (5), *Sixième* (6), *Septième* (7) and *Huitième* (8). The two lowest score three and four points respectively; the higher Sequences score ten more than their component cards (e.g., *Quint* fifteen, *Sixième* sixteen, etc.).

Here, again, the longest Sequence is the only one to score and when of equal length, only the higher; thus a Sixième to the K beats a Sixième to the Q. Furthermore, a longer Sequence, even though composed of low cards, say, a Quint to the Jack, takes precedence of *any* shorter Sequence, even a Quart Major (Four to the Ace).

If both players have Sequences of equal length and value, neither side scores for Sequence, even though one or both hold inferior Sequences as well. Thus if Y has a Quint Major (Five to the Ace) in Spades and Z a Quint Major in Hearts, the fact that Y has also, let us say, a good Tierce is ignored; but a player scoring a Sequence counts any inferior Sequence held, even though it may not be as good as an intermediate Sequence in his opponent's hand. Thus, if Y has a Sixième to the K and two Tierces in his hand as well, while Z has only a Sixième to the Q, Y is entitled to score for all his Sequences, while Z scores nothing for his.

QUATORZES AND TRIOS. A *Quatorze* is a combination of four of a kind higher than a Nine (such as Four Aces or Four Kings) and, if good, counts fourteen. A *Trio* is a similar combination of three, also higher than a Nine, which, if good, counts three. The player holding the highest Quatorze is entitled to score any other Quatorzes he may hold, as well as all his Trios. The lowest Quatorze (Four Tens) is better than the highest Trio. Thus, if Y holds Four Tens and Z Three Aces, Kings and Queens, Z's excellent holding scores nothing.

DISCARDING. The players, bearing the combinations in mind, will look at their cards and sort them into suits. Unless there is a freak distribution each will find one or more "gaps" in his hand. Thus—the Elder Hand may have three Aces out of the four and a long suit needing only one card for a Sequence. This is where the Stock comes in. As the top five cards are his, he may discard up to five and substitute the corresponding number from these, taking them in order. He must exchange at least one card, and he is entitled to look at any of the five. Skilful discarding is one of the most important features in the game, as it enables an indifferent hand to be turned into a valuable one, and the novice will soon learn by experience what to throw away and what to save for. In the case indicated above, Elder Hand will naturally try to complete his Sequence and to draw for the missing Ace.

When the Elder Hand has completed his discarding it is the turn of the dealer, who may take all the cards left by Elder Hand as well as his own three. He must exchange at least one card, and he may look at all cards he leaves in the Stock, and when Elder Hand has led to the first trick he too may look at any cards remaining in the Stock.

DECLARING. The hands are now complete and the scoring begins, before any cards are actually played. Elder Hand in our example finds that, thanks to his discarding, he has completed his Sequence though he has failed to draw the fourth Ace, which was all the time in his opponent's hand. He now holds, let us say, five Clubs in Sequence to the Q, Ace, Q, J, 10 of Diamonds, Ace of Spades and Ace of Hearts. Dealer, who had an indifferent hand, has managed in the course of his discarding to collect a Sequence of Four (Quart) and a Quatorze of Four Kings.

Elder Hand begins by saying " Point of Five, five," indicating his five Clubs, whereupon Dealer, who has only a Point of Four, says " Good." If Dealer also had a Point of Five, the respective pip-values would be counted to decide who scores. If the respective pip-values proved equal, Dealer's response would have been " Equal," and neither side would have scored for Point. If Dealer had a Point of Six or better, he would have replied " Not good."

Elder Hand next claims his Sequence of Five by saying " Quint, twenty," i.e., five for the Point and fifteen for the Quint. Dealer again says " Good," as he cannot do better than a Sequence of Four (Quart). Elder Hand, having established his superior Sequence, now claims three more points for his Tierce in Diamonds —twenty-three.

He next claims for his Trio of Aces, but here, Dealer having a Quatorze of Kings, says " Not good."

This finishes the preliminary scoring as far as Elder Hand is concerned. Before, however, going on to the play of the hands it is necessary to mention that if either player scores thirty points before play starts and all his declarations are good he is entitled to add sixty for *Repique*. And " equal " Point does not save Repique, but Carte Blanche does. A player may not call out of the correct order of the cards in order to obtain Repique.

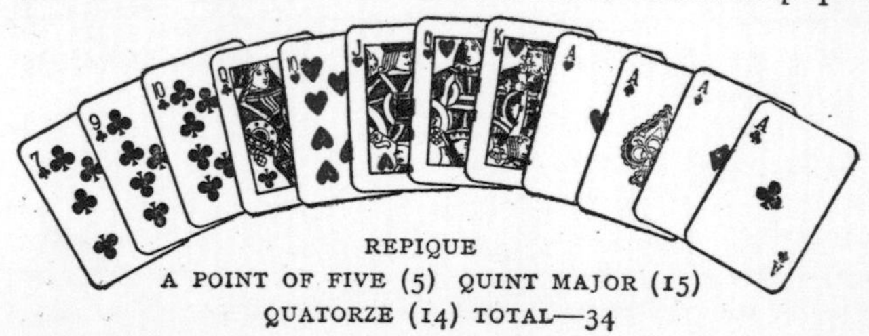

REPIQUE
A POINT OF FIVE (5) QUINT MAJOR (15)
QUATORZE (14) TOTAL—34

PLAY OF THE CARDS—Elder Hand leads any card he likes and counts one for the lead. In our example, having already scored twenty-three he adds his one and says "Twenty-four." Dealer, before playing to the card led, must declare any combination of his own that is better than his opponent's—in our example a Quartorze of Kings—fourteen. Dealer must follow suit, but he is not obliged to win the trick. The tricks are left face upwards on the table and may be examined at any time.

If Elder Hand wins his lead he leads again, and again counts one. If Dealer wins the trick he counts one for winning and one more for leading to the following trick.

If Elder Hand can reach thirty by his scores for combinations and by his leads in actual play before Dealer has scored anything, he is entitled to add thirty for *Pique*, and he takes this score even though he loses the trick by which he reaches thirty. Since the right to lead carries with it one point Dealer can never score Pique.

The winner of the last trick scores two points instead of one. The player winning most tricks scores ten for the *Cards*, but if both win six tricks, neither scores for Cards. If a player wins all twelve tricks he scores forty for *Capot*, instead of ten.

GAME—A *Partie* consists of six deals, and is won by the player making the higher aggregate score. In the event of a tie each deals once more, and that hand having been played, the game is over—even if a second tie results.

The winner of the Partie deducts the loser's score from his own and adds one hundred for Game. If the loser fails to score a hundred he is RUBICONED, and the winner adds the loser's score to his own, in addition to the hundred.

PIQUET AU CENT

The older form of Piquet is very similar to the current game, the main difference being in the scoring. There is no Rubicon, and the game is one hundred up. By way of compensation for the absence of the Rubicon, if a player fails to reach fifty when his opponent has scored a hundred he is *Lurched*, and loses a double game.

There are also some minor differences. In cutting, the lower (not the higher) card gives the right to deal. The cards are dealt two at a time, never three at a time. The Dealer need not discard at all, although Elder Hand is obliged, as in the standard game, to discard at least one card. If Dealer has Carte Blanche, he need not declare it until his opponent has discarded. In claiming Sequence a player must state the top card of his Sequence ; and in claiming Quatorzes or Trios he must always state the value of the cards in respect of which he claims.

Three-handed Piquet

There are two methods of conducting the game when three players take part, the more popular being Chouette.

Chouette—The players first cut and the highest (say X) has the deal and choice of seats, and plays against the next highest (say Y), while Z, who has cut the lowest card, sits out and advises Y.

If X wins the first Partie he next plays Z, and Y sits out as Z's adviser ; if X wins again Y and Z change places once more ; and so on until X loses, when his late opponent (say Y) takes his place and plays the other member (in this case Z), X becoming the adviser of Z. A corresponding interchange of occupations takes place (as before between X and Z) with every succeeding Partie until Y loses, when Z plays against X and Y in the same manner. As soon as Z loses, the game reverts to the original position, with X opposing Y and Z.

Three-handed—In this form of the game all play simultaneously, the player winning the deal dealing ten cards to each, leaving only two in the Stock, which he alone is entitled to exchange.

Player on Dealer's left declares first. The limit for Repique and Pique is twenty (instead of thirty) and the bonuses seventy and forty (instead of sixty and thirty).

The player winning most cards adds ten (five in the case of a tie). Capot counts forty if all the tricks are taken by one player; if two players share the cards they score twenty each.

FOUR-HANDED PIQUET

The players cut for partners, the two lowest playing the two highest. Lowest deals, and partners sit opposite each other. All the cards are dealt, so that each player has eight cards, and there is no Stock.

The player on the left of the Dealer declares everything he has (not one item at a time) and then leads a card without waiting for a response. The second player next declares his hand and admits as "good" or rejects as "not good" any, or all, of the first player's declarations. The third and fourth players do the same. A player may score inferior combinations if his partner's declarations are good. Thus, for example, if Y and Z are partners and Y has a Quatorze of Four Aces, Z is allowed to declare a Quatorze or Trio of Kings, Queens, etc., to the exclusion of any Quatorze or Trio in the hands of the other partners, A and B. Similarly, if A has declared a "good" Quint (Sequence of five) his partner may declare a Tierce to the exclusion of any Sequences in the hands of Y and Z. As soon as the first trick is won the hands are shown and the respective claims verified.

Repique and Pique count as in Three-Handed Piquet, with the additional advantage that they can be scored either by a player alone or between two partners.

IMPERIAL PIQUET

Imperial Piquet differs from all other variations in that it is played with a trump suit and counters are used. There are no discards.

The cards rank K, Q, J, Ace, 10, 9, 8, 7. The K, Q, J, Ace and 7 of trumps are Honours.

COUNTERS. Each player has six white and four red

counters, the red being equal to six white. He places them on his left and scores by moving a red or white counter to his right. The player who first moves all his counters thus wins the game.

DEALING. Twelve cards are dealt to each, as in the standard game, and the twenty-fifth is turned up for trumps.

IMPÉRIALES. An *impériale* consists of Four Kings, Queens, Jacks, Aces or 7s in one hand, or of a Sequence of K, Q, J, Ace (also in one hand) and scores six; Carte Blanche is a *Double Impériale,* scoring twelve. Trios are disregarded in this game, as also are Four 8s, 9s, or 10s.

A Sequence may be claimed by the Dealer if the turn-up completes his Sequence *(Impériale de Retourne)*, or by either player taking his opponent's J or Ace and thereby completing his own Sequence *(Impériale Tombée).*

DECLARING. Point counts one. If either Point or Sequence is equal, Elder Hand scores it.

PLAY OF THE HAND. The second player must win the trick if he can, either with a higher card of the same suit or with a trump. Each honour won in play counts one. The winner of the *Cards* (majority of tricks) scores one for each odd trick. Capot counts twelve. When a player has made six in white counters, he exchanges them for a red counter and his opponent must move back to his left all the white counters that he has moved up.

BÉZIQUE

THERE are many card games for two players, but only Piquet and Bézique have preserved their evergreen freshness. Of the two, Piquet is, perhaps, the more scientific, but Bézique may claim to be more popular. In spite of its somewhat elaborate rules Bézique is a comparatively easy game to play. It demands just enough concentration to be interesting, while it can never be sublimated into an ordeal.

The many attempts at improving the original game have not succeeded in dislodging it from the position which it still occupies in the affections of card-players. They have, however, given rise to a number of varieties, the normal game being that first described here.

BÉZIQUE is a game for two persons. It is played with two packs of cards of which all cards up to and including the six have been removed—in other words, the Piquet pack of 32 cards is duplicated. The backs of the two packs should be identical. The total number of cards is 64—16 cards of each suit. Thus there are two Aces, two Kings, two Queens, etc., of each suit, or eight Aces, eight Kings, eight Queens, etc., altogether.

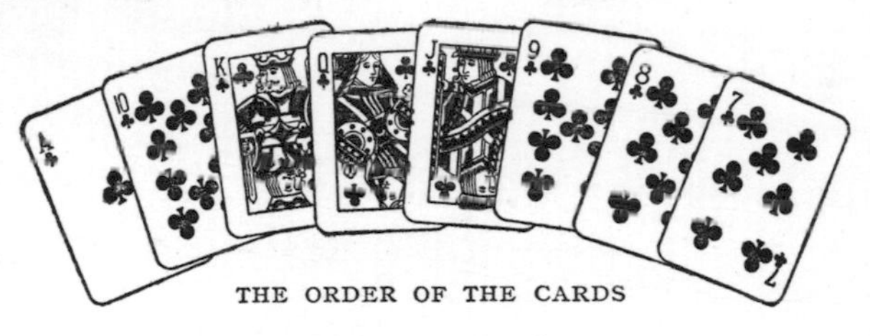

THE ORDER OF THE CARDS

CUTTING. The cards are shuffled, and the player drawing the higher card deals. The ranking of the cards is unusual, viz., Ace, Ten, King, Queen, Jack, Nine, Eight, Seven; and the same order is used for cutting as for play.

DEALING. The cards are cut, and the dealer, reuniting the two halves of the pack, deals eight cards to his opponent and eight to himself—three at a time, then two at a time, then three at a time. The seventeenth card is turned face upwards on the table between the players, and indicates trumps, i.e., the suit of the seventeenth card is the trump suit for that deal. The undealt remainder, called the "stock," is placed face downwards on the table next to the turned-up card (called the "turn-up"). Each player deals in turn after each hand.

OBJECT OF THE GAME. To score by declaring certain cards or combinations of cards, and (this is important as it is sometimes forgotten) to prevent, as far as possible, the adversary from scoring. The player first reaching the agreed limit (usually 2,000; but any thousand from 1,000 to 10,000) wins the game.

SCORES

A.	Four Aces	100
B.	Four Kings	80
C.	Four Queens	60
D.	Four Jacks	40
E.	Marriage	20
F.	Royal Marriage	40
G.	Bézique	40
H.	Double Bézique	500
I.	Sequence in Trumps	250
J.	Seven of Trumps, turned up ...	10
K.	Seven of Trumps, declared ...	10
L.	Seven of Trumps, exchanged ...	10
M.	Last Trick	10
N.	Aces and Tens, each	10

Markers are usually supplied with complete packs of Bézique cards.

EXPLANATION OF SCORES

A-D. The four cards making up a combination of Aces, Kings, Queens or Jacks may be of any suit, duplicates being immaterial. Thus four Kings may be two Hearts, one Diamond and one Club; four Queens, one of each suit; four Jacks, two Hearts and two Diamonds; or any other combination. The declarer of any of these sets of four may not use any of them again to make the same declaration, but he may if he draws the other four Kings, Queens, or Jacks, declare a second set of four. This means that if a player has declared, for instance, four Kings, and then plays one of his declared Kings, he is not allowed, on drawing a fifth King, to add it to his three remaining Kings and score four Kings again.

E. MARRIAGE, often known as COMMON MARRIAGE, is the declaration of K or Q in any one of the three suits that do not happen to be trumps.

F. ROYAL MARRIAGE, so called to distinguish it from the marriage of commoners, is the declaration of K and Q of trumps.

It should be noted, both in the case of a Royal and a Common Marriage, that widowed spouses may not remarry. A player, remembering that there are two Kings and two Queens in each suit, might otherwise be tempted, after having declared, say, K and Q of Hearts, and having played the K, to join the second K of Hearts to the widowed Q and claim a second Marriage. There is nothing, however, to prevent him, if he is fortunate enough to draw both the second K and the second Q of Hearts, declaring another Marriage in that suit.

G. BÉZIQUE is the declaration of Q of Spades and J of Diamonds, or, when either Spades or Diamonds are trumps, the declaration of Q of Clubs and J of Hearts. A variation of the game is to keep to the Q of Spades and J of Diamonds whatever the trumps; this greatly simplifies the play of a hand whenever Spades or Diamonds are trumps. The reason for this is obvious. If either Spades or Diamonds are trumps, one of the Bézique cards must also be one of the sequence cards, so that the player's hand becomes easier to play. It should be noted that the fact that a Q of Spades (or Clubs) has entered into an irregular union with a J does not prevent her lawful marriage to a K (see p. 87 DECLARING).

H. Double Bézique is simultaneous declaration of two Queens of Spades (or Clubs ; see G., p. 85) and two Jacks of Diamonds (or Hearts). If Bézique has already been declared, the score for Double Bézique is added ; total 540 ; but if Bézique has not already been declared, only the score for Double Bézique is allowed.

Note.—*(a)* If either of the cards composing the original declaration of Bézique has been played, Double Bézique may not be scored, as all four cards must be on the table together ; but a second Single Bézique may be scored with the second pair of cards.

(b) Neither of the cards composing the first Bézique may be used to declare the second Bézique. This, of course, is in accordance with the rule governing Marriages (see p. 85).

I. Sequence in Trumps is declaration of Ace, Ten, King, Queen, Jack in trumps. In order to count Royal Marriage (K and Q in trumps) as well as Sequence, Royal Marriage must be declared first. If Sequence is declared first, the score for Royal Marriage may not be made ; although if the player draws the second royal pair he may declare Royal Marriage with it. Normally, Sequence will be the addition of Ace, Ten, Jack to the Royal Marriage already declared.

J. The dealer is given a bonus of 10 if the turn-up is a Seven.

K. The Seven of Trumps may be declared after winning a trick (see Declaring, p. 87).

L. The chances are greatly in favour of the turn-up being a higher card than the Seven. It may be a sequence card (Ace, Ten, King, Queen, Jack). The winner of a trick (see Declaring) is entitled, if holding either Seven of Trumps, to exchange it for the turn-up. This he does by taking the turn-up into his own hand and placing the Seven of Trumps in its place on the table.

M. Last Trick is strictly the last trick but eight. It is the last trick taken before the stock is exhausted. As one side or other must score this, the Last Trick counts 20 on a division.

N. Aces and Tens (technically known as Brisques). When all cards have been played, including the last eight tricks (see p. 91), each side counts the number of

Aces and Tens in the tricks that he has taken. For each Ace and each Ten he counts ten. Sometimes brisques are scored as they are made; but this method of scoring them is not recommended.

Declaring. No declaration may be made until the player has won a trick (see below, Trick Winning). The declared card or combination of cards is placed face upwards on the table in front of the player declaring. It counts as an integral part of his hand, and the cards may be played in the same manner as the cards remaining in his hand.

As a corollary to this rule, the exchanged card (see Scores, L) may not be used to form a declaration until a second trick has been taken.

The same card may figure in two different declarations, the Q of Spades for example, may form part of a Marriage and, after the winning of a second trick, may form part of a Bézique; or a King may form part of a marriage and subsequently part of a set of four Kings. Only one declaration may be made at a time in respect of the same card. The order is immaterial, except in the case of Double Bézique or Sequence (see p. 86, Scores, H and I).

Two or more declarations may be made simultaneously, provided the same card is not involved; thus the winner of a trick may declare a Royal Marriage and a Common Marriage, and exchange the Seven of Trumps.

Trick Winning. A trick is won by taking the adversary's card, either with a higher card *of the same suit* or with a trump. Thus if a player leads a Seven of Hearts and his opponent plays Ace of Clubs (not being trumps) the Seven of Hearts wins whether it is a trump or not. It should not be forgotten that the Ten takes every card in its suit except the Ace. When the trick is won it is turned and placed face downwards on the table in front of the winner. Subsequent tricks are placed on the top of the first trick—tricks are not kept distinct, as in bridge or whist. Each heap of tricks must be kept distinct, as at the end of the game the heaps are examined in order that the Aces and Tens contained therein may be counted (see p. 86, Scores, N). If two cards of the same value are played (e.g., if the second player plays the other Eight of Spades to the first Eight of Spades), the led card wins.

Replenishing the Hand. After a trick has been won each player has only seven cards left. First the winner, then the loser draws a card from the stock, and this goes on until the Last Trick. The winner of the Last Trick takes the remaining card from the stock and the loser the turn-up (or the exchanged Seven). Thus the number of cards in each player's hand is kept constant throughout the first part of the game.

Play of the Hands

A. From the Deal to the Last Trick

1. The non-dealer leads. In subsequent tricks the winner of the previous trick leads.

2. The second player may play any card he likes. It is not necessary to follow suit, but a trick cannot be taken unless the second player follows suit or trumps (see p. 87, Trick Winning).

3. Unless you wish to declare, to make sure of an Ace or Ten, or to take your opponent's Ace or Ten, it is advisable not to take the trick. If you continue to let your opponent take the tricks he will, sooner or later, be obliged to play an Ace or Ten, which you can then take with a small trump (or with the appropriate Ace).

4. Keep your small trumps for taking your opponent's Aces or Tens and for taking a trick when you want to do so. There are only six of them, two Sevens, two Eights and two Nines. Notice how many have been played. If all are accounted for you can play an Ace or Ten with more confidence, as it cannot then be taken except by a valuable card.

5. Do not lose Aces or Tens if you can help it. They count 20 each on a division—i.e., if you do not take them your opponent will (but see p. 90, para. 11). Do not lead an Ace or Ten if you can help it. It sometimes pays, however, if you have to play an Ace or Ten and

you find your opponent cannot take it, to play another, as it shows that he is in difficulties. He is obviously saving for one or more declarations and he may not have a trump or an Ace to spare. He may even have to throw a brisque on to yours, when you will gain 20 (40 on a division).

6. Always aim at the highest scores, e.g., Double Bézique, Sequence, Four Kings, etc., with one exception. Unless you already have three Aces it is not wise normally to save for Four Aces, in preference to Four Kings or Four Queens, in spite of the higher value of the Aces, as Kings and Queens can marry and Aces cannot. Furthermore, you may obtain your declaration of four Aces and then lose every one of them to your opponent's trumps. You will then gain 100 for Four Aces and lose 40 (or 80 on a division) for the trumped Aces—net gain only 20. It is much wiser, therefore, to use your Aces for taking tricks.

7. The fascination of the game is due to the necessity for exercising judgement and making wise decisions. You will very soon find that you cannot save for everything, as you have only eight cards in your hand. A Sequence takes up five cards and a combination of Four Kings four cards. You will, therefore, be faced with the choice of saving for one or the other, though—if you are lucky—you may make both scores, one after the other. It is necessary, therefore, to watch your opponent's play. If he throws a King he may be saving for Queens, and it will pay you not to save for Queens as well; for unless the eight are equally divided between the two hands, you cannot both score Four Queens. If your opponent, having declared Four Queens, plays a fifth, you must realise at once that it is impossible in that hand for you to score Four Queens too. Unless, therefore, your Queens are to be used for Bézique or Marriages, they have become worthless and should be discarded.

8. Continue to watch the play of your opponent. If, in declaring, for example, Four Kings, he puts down two Kings of trumps, you must realise at once that your chances of Sequence are gone. The play of your

own hand will then be easier, as you will not have to cling to Sequence cards if you want to declare something else. If your opponent plays either of the Bézique cards you cannot make Double Bézique. If he plays a Sequence card, the Ten of trumps for example, he probably has the duplicate, but in this case you must be on your guard against bluffing. It may be a ruse to induce you to part with your own Sequence cards.

9. If you can possibly avoid giving information during the play of your own hand you will make things much more difficult for your opponent. If you have, for instance, two Kings of trumps and two other Kings, try, if possible, to wait for a fifth King (unless the score is critical; see below, para. 11) and conceal the duplicate. It is vitally important to conceal a Bézique card if you think your opponent has the other three, as by so doing you make him hang on to his now worthless Bézique cards and lose the chance of declaring Sequence, Four Kings, etc. In other words he will be buoyed up with false hope and end by declaring practically nothing.

10. Unless the score is critical—you want, for instance, only 40 or 50 for game, do not bother to save for Four Jacks, as they may prevent you from making far more valuable declarations. It is definitely inadvisable to declare Four Jacks if any of them is a Bézique or trump card, especially if two of them are trump cards, as this is giving information to the enemy (see above, para. 9).

11. When you are nearing the end of the game, i.e., if you require only 100 or so—

(a) Make a score that will take you out—Sequence or Double Bézique, for instance—without waiting to score the minor score of Royal Marriage or Single Bézique. This is especially important if your opponent is also approaching game.

(b) Do not trouble about Aces and Tens, as the game will probably have been lost and won before you reach the counting of these.

12. If you have Sequence in your hand and three

cards towards Double Bézique, it is tempting to sacrifice the chance of Double Bézique in order to score for Sequence. Unless, however, the state of the score demands otherwise, you should sacrifice one of your Sequence cards as you may draw the duplicate. If you sacrifice one of your Double Bézique cards you have lost all chance of making it until the next hand.

13. Nearing the end of the hand, if it appears that both sides are saving for a high score, e.g., Sequence or Double Bézique, it is better, if you have not a chance of declaring yourself, to sacrifice your own high cards in the attempt to prevent the adversary from scoring. If, for example, you play a Jack of trumps, your opponent cannot take it except with a higher sequence card, and unless he has a duplicate you wreck his chances of making Sequence. Do not, however, start this play too soon; if you do, you may have used up all your good cards in vain.

14. If you have a Sequence card (say Ten of trumps) in your hand and the turn-up is the same Sequence card, take the first opportunity of exchanging the Seven if you are fortunate enough to draw it. This will effectively prevent your opponent from scoring Sequence. It would even pay to take the trick with your own Ten of trumps (if you have no other card available) and exchange the Seven at once, as your opponent may have the other Seven. This, however, would be giving information to the enemy.

B. Last Eight Tricks

1. After the "Last Trick" has been played each player gathers up his eight cards, including declared cards on the table, and the remaining cards are played until they are all gone. The sole object of this part of the game is to score the remaining Aces and Tens. No declarations may be made.

2. The winner of the Last Trick leads. The opponent must now follow suit or trump. He must take the trick

if he can, under the penalty of surrendering all the Aces and Tens left in his hand. He may not trump, however, if he has any card of the suit led. No score is made for what is actually the last trick.

3. You should watch the declared cards of your opponent, before he gathers them up. This may allow you to lead an Ace with confidence if it is the same suit as one of these cards.

4. If you think you have more trump cards than your opponent play all your trumps out. If you exhaust his trumps you will secure your Aces and possibly your Tens as well.

5. If you cannot do this and find that your opponent is short of a particular suit, lead a worthless card of that suit as often as you can, as it will make him use up his trumps to no good purpose.

RUBICON BÉZIQUE

Rubicon Bézique is a modification of ordinary Bézique and has been honoured with a Code of Laws framed by a committee of the Portland Club. It therefore has some claim to be regarded as the standard game, but it is doubtful if it has replaced the older game in popularity. The chief (possibly the only) drawback is the physical difficulty of managing a pack of 128 cards.

The game, which, like its progenitor, is one for two players, is very similar to ordinary Bézique, but:

1. Four Bézique packs of 32 cards are required instead of two, the combined 128 cards comprising 16 each of Aces, Tens, Kings, Queens, Jacks, Nines, Eights and Sevens.

2. Nine cards are dealt instead of eight (by three, three, and three, or one at a time).

3. There is no turn-up, consequently the peculiar value of the Seven disappears, and there is no score for turning-up, exchanging, or declaring it.

4. The game is completed in one hand.

5. The scores are the same as in ordinary Bézique

(apart from the disappearance of the Seven) with the following additions :

(a)	A player declaring Carte Blanche	scores	50
(b)	,, ,, Ordinary Sequence	,,	150
(c)	,, ,, Triple Bézique	,,	1500
(d)	,, ,, Quadruple Bézique	,,	4500
(e)	The winner of the Last Trick	,,	50

Explanation of Scores

(a) Carte Blanche. If either dealer or pone (non-dealer) is dealt a hand containing no K, Q or J, he is entitled at the start of the game to declare Carte Blanche. This he does by showing all his cards, one after the other, on the table. He then scores 50 and picks up his hand, and the game proceeds. Note that the possession of Aces, Tens, or of Aces and Tens does not affect the validity of the claim, and that there is nothing to prevent both players from declaring Carte Blanche although this is most unlikely to happen.

If the declarer of Carte Blanche, after playing to the first trick and drawing from the stock, draws another card which is not a K, Q or J, he is entitled to make the declaration a second time. He may go on doing this until he draws a K, Q or J, but the first of these drawn puts a stop to this source of scoring.

Carte Blanche is the only instance in Rubicon of a score being made without winning a trick. In every other case, as in ordinary Bézique, no declaration is valid until the declarer has won a trick.

(b) Ordinary Sequence, or Sequence in Plain Suits, is a combination of Ace, Ten, K, Q and J in any of the three suits that do not happen to be trumps.

(c) Triple Bézique is the simultaneous declaration of three Queens of Spades and three Jacks of Diamonds (or three Queens of Clubs and three Jacks of Hearts : see Bézique). Normally the player wishing to declare this will already have declared both Single and Double Bézique, and will add the third Q and J to the Double Bézique previously declared. If he declares Triple

Bézique without waiting to declare the inferior combinations he forfeits all claim to score for the inferior combinations. In other words, instead of scoring 40 (Bézique) plus 500 (Double Bézique) plus 1,500 (Triple Bézique), amounting to 2,040, all he may declare is 1,500.

(d) QUADRUPLE BÉZIQUE. This, the greatest prize of the game, is naturally the most difficult to obtain. It consists in declaring simultaneously all four Queens of Spades (or Clubs) and all four Jacks of Diamonds (or Hearts). The rule about inferior combinations holds good here also. If the player has progressed through all the Bézique stages he will have scored 40 plus 500 plus 1,500 plus 4,500—6,540 in all; and with this huge score he is practically certain to win the game. It is therefore highly worth while to aim at Quadruple Bézique if there is a reasonable chance of obtaining it.

(e) LAST TRICK. As one side or the other must win this, it is always advisable to try to score it. It makes a difference of 100 to the score.

6. As there is no turn-up, trumps are determined by the suit of the first Marriage declared by either player. If, however, a Sequence is declared first, the suit of the Sequence becomes trumps; but in view of the rule about forfeiting the score for an inferior combination, a player is not likely to declare Sequence before declaring his Marriage.

7. There is a slight difference in the play of the hand. Instead of each player gathering his trick at once, the played cards remain on the table until a BRISQUE (Ace or Ten) is played.

8. If a card forming part of the combination is played, leaving the combination defective, the defect may be made good by substituting another card of the appropriate rank. Thus, if a player has declared Four Kings and plays one of them, leaving only three Kings on the table, he is entitled, on drawing a fifth King from the stock, to make good his Four Kings and score over again. This is directly contrary to the procedure in ordinary Bézique.

As a corollary to this rule, if a player has declared

two Marriages in the same suit he is entitled to re-arrange the spouses and declare two more Marriages in that suit with the four cards lying on the table.

9. LAST NINE TRICKS. These are played in the same way as the Last Eight Tricks in ordinary Bézique.

10. FINAL SCORING. It is in the final computation that the Rubicon comes in, but only in certain circumstances.

Normally, the player scoring most points deducts the loser's score from his own (fractions of a hundred being disregarded and any difference less than a hundred being counted as a hundred), and 500 is added for game. Thus, if Y has scored 1,720, and Z 1,710, Y is entitled to score 100, the difference of 10 in the respective scores being regarded as 100, which, with the 500 for game, gives him a score of 600.

Brisques are, as a rule, disregarded, but if the scores are equal, it is—normally—necessary to count them; the player scoring most then computes his score in the manner indicated above. Thus, if both Y and Z have tied with 2,300, and, after the brisques have been counted it is found that Y has 220 to score for brisques and Z only 100, Y becomes the winner. If there is still a tie after the brisques have been counted, i.e., each player has 16 brisques (there are, of course, 32 of them altogether), the game is drawn.

We now come to the RUBICON itself—this is the name for the score of 1,000, and forms the most critical period in the game.

If the loser's score is less than 1,000 (whether the winner's exceeds this figure or not) the loser is in danger of being "Rubiconed," that is to say—the winner takes the loser's score as well as his own (still disregarding fractions of 100) and adds 1,300 (not 500) to his score for the game. Thus if Y has scored 2,670 and Z only 990, Y takes 2,600 plus 900 (3,500) which, with the 1,300 for game, gives him the respectable total of 4,800. There is a still further penalty for the ultra-unfortunate (or extremely careless) player, for if the loser has scored less than 100—a most unlikely eventuality—the winner adds an extra 100 to his score. There is, however, one mitigation to this drastic law and heavy penalty, for, in order to give one a chance of "saving the Rubicon," brisques are counted. If, after this has been done, the loser's score exceeds 1,000, he is not "Rubiconed," and the computation proceeds on normal lines. Thus, if Y has scored 2,670 and Z only 840, and the addition of the brisques brings the respective scores to 2,820 and 1,010, the danger to Z is averted.

If, however, brisques have already been taken into account to decide the winner of a tie and it is found that the loser is "Rubiconed," the brisques, although counted to decide the winner, are not added to the scores. Thus, if Y and Z tie with 980, and it appears that Y has more brisques than Z, Y becomes the winner and Z is "Rubiconed." The fortunate Y then adds Z's 900 to his own 900, making 1,800, to which he adds the 1,300 for game, thus reaching a total of 3,100.

A short examination of this somewhat intricate method of scoring will show how exceedingly important it is to avoid being "Rubiconed." When the scores are nearly equal, the winning or losing of a single Ace or Ten may make a difference of 3,000 points, as in the example given immediately above.

POLISH BÉZIQUE

Polish Bézique is a pleasing variation of the ordinary game for two players, and is quite easy to master.

The rules governing rank, cutting, dealing, and playing the cards are as in "straight" Bézique, and the scoring is similar (though there is a slight difference in the method of scoring brisques); but the difference in the disposal of the played cards, and in the declaration of combinations is fundamental.

To take first the first of these two fundamental differences:

Disposal of Played Cards. All played cards of no combination value are turned and quitted as in ordinary Bézique, but the others are placed face upwards, by the winner of each trick, in groups of Aces, Kings, Queens and Jacks, with two exceptions. The Ten of trumps is placed face upwards by itself in readiness for Sequence; or if it is the only card required to complete a Sequence, it is used at once to declare that combination. The Seven of Trumps is, by its winner, either exchanged for the turn-up or declared in the manner detailed later in this article. Its combination value is merely indirect in that it is used to obtain a valuable turn-up. The latter card, if an Ace, K, Q or J, is placed (by the player exchanging the Seven of Trumps) in its proper place among the Aces, Kings, Queens or Jacks; if a Ten it is placed as indicated above. The cards thus arranged are called *Open Cards*, and may not be played to a trick—a method of procedure which forms an important variation from ordinary Bézique.

We can now turn to the declaration of combinations. A declaration is made by adding a card won in a trick to any of the Open Cards with which it forms a combination. Thus if Y has three "open" Kings on the table and wins a trick containing a fourth K (either by playing a winning K out of his own hand or by taking his opponent's K with a higher card), he is entitled to declare Four Kings.

As many declarations as are possible must be made at the same time. Thus, if Spades are trumps, and Y has won a Q of trumps with his K and has already on the table the following Open Cards—three other Q's, the Ace, Ten, and J of trumps, and the J of Diamonds, then, assuming that the cards composing Bézique remain Q of Spades and J of Diamonds, whatever the trumps (see BÉZIQUE, p. 84) he scores simultaneously:

Royal Marriage	40
Four Queens	60
Sequence	250
Bézique	40
Total	390

If a player fails to score the maximum number of combinations possible on adding the card just won to the Open Cards, he forfeits his chance of scoring them, for the rule is that a declaration must include a card played to the trick just won.

A second declaration of the same category may not be made if it involves using the same cards. Thus, if Y has declared Four Queens, he is not entitled, on winning a fifth Q, to declare Four Queens again. Similarly, a K or Q once married may not be married again. There is nothing, however, to prevent Y, if he is lucky enough to win all eight Q's, from declaring a second combination of Four Q's with the second batch of four. Similarly, if after having declared, for instance, Marriage of K and Q of Clubs, he wins the second K and Q of Clubs, he is in order in declaring the second Marriage in that suit.

SEVEN OF TRUMPS. As we have already mentioned, it is the *winner* of the trick containing this card who is entitled to exchange or to declare it, not the holder (unless he is also the winner). Thus, if Y plays the Seven of trumps and Z takes it with the Eight (or any higher card) of trumps, it is Z, not Y, who exchanges or declares the Seven. When the Seven has been declared it is turned and added to the worthless cards, as it now becomes valueless.

BRISQUES (Aces and Tens) are counted as soon as won, not at the end of the game (as in ordinary Bézique).

When we arrive at the LAST EIGHT TRICKS, play is the same as in Bézique, except that declarations continue to be made with the cards that are won. The only exception to this rule is that the Seven of trumps, if forming part of the hand of the loser of the Last Trick, as a result of having been turned up or exchanged, may not be declared by the player winning it. The reason for this is, of course, that the Seven has already been used to score, and may not be so used again.

GAME. As the scoring is much higher than in ordinary Bézique, the Game points are usually doubled, that is, it takes 4,000 instead of 2,000 to score Game.

FOUR-HANDED BÉZIQUE

There are two varieties of this game, Four-handed Bézique played according to the rules of ordinary Bézique, and Four-handed Bézique played according to the rules of Rubicon Bézique. The latter (which has been fortified with a Code of Laws drawn up by the Portland Club) is the official game. We will deal with the unofficial game first.

UNOFFICIAL FOUR-HANDED BÉZIQUE. Four packs of 32 Bézique cards are required (128 cards altogether) and play is usually between partners, though it is permissible to play "all against all."

In the partnership game the declarer may either declare his own hand or combine his partner's declared cards with his own to form scoring combinations. If the winner of a trick is unable or unwilling to declare he passes the right of declaration to his partner, with the words "I leave it to you, partner."

The scores are the same as in ordinary Bézique, with the addition of Triple Bézique, which scores 1,500. Quadruple Bézique (though possible in a partnership game) is not scored. The game points are double those in ordinary Bézique (usually 4,000).

OFFICIAL FOUR-HANDED BÉZIQUE. As the main principles of Rubicon Bézique apply to Four-Handed Bézique of the official variety, the reader should first make himself a master of them (see pp. 92-96).

Six packs of 32 Bézique cards are required, or 192 cards in all. Thus there are 24 cards of each separate value, viz., Aces, Tens, Kings, Queens, Jacks, Nines, Eights and Sevens. If the players have found the 128 cards of Rubicon Bézique difficult to shuffle, they may find the 192 cards of the four-handed game well-nigh unmanageable, unless they do as is usual in both these cases and shuffle as many as may be conveniently handled at a time, finally rejoining the various handfuls.

The players cut for partners, and the two lowest play against the two highest. If two equal cards are cut the players concerned must cut again; but we should note here that in view of the great number of duplicate cards (6 of every denomination, or 24, including all four suits), it is perhaps better for the players to make a private arrangement about partners, for in the absence of this, cutting may take some considerable time. The player cutting the lowest card is the dealer, and partners arrange themselves as in bridge or whist.

DEALING. The dealer deals 24 cards, face downwards, on top of each other. On these he places a card of a larger size and different pattern, called the *Divider*. He then deals nine cards to each player, and places the remaining 132 cards on the top of the Divider; this undealt residue is called the Stock. The sole object of the Divider is to enable the players when nearing the end of the game to know how many cards are left in the Stock. It is not absolutely necessary.

If a player is dealt a hand containing no K, Q or J, he may claim *Carte Blanche*, as in Rubicon Bézique (see p. 93).

If a player and his partner are both dealt hands containing no K, Q or J, the partners may claim *Double Carte Blanche*. If in the next draw from the Stock one partner draws a K, Q or J, and the other partner does not, the side may claim a further *Single Carte Blanche*. If both partners fail to draw a K, Q or J, the side may claim another *Double Carte Blanche*. Scoring from this source goes on until both partners have drawn a K, Q or J.

LEADING. The player on the left of the dealer leads, and the others play clock-wise, as in bridge or whist.

SCORES are the same as in Rubicon Bézique, with the following additions and alterations:

Carte Blanche	... ...	counts	100
Double Carte Blanche	... ...	,,	500
Quintuple Bézique*	... ...	,,	13,500
Four Aces	(all trumps) ...	,,	1,000
Four Tens	do. ...	,,	900

* Sextuple Bézique, which is, of course, possible, is so rare that no score is allotted to it.

Four Kings	(all trumps)	... counts	800
Four Queens	do.	... ,,	600
Four Jacks	do.	... ,,	400

A note or two on this list of scores may be useful. *Quintuple Bézique,* the greatest prize of the game, consists of the simultaneous declaration of Five Queens of Spades (or Clubs) and Five Jacks of Diamonds (or Hearts).

The introduction of combinations of four, or *Quartettes,* all in trumps, is new. A Quartette of trump cards counts *ten times* as much as a Quartette of assorted cards.

Four Tens is peculiar to the four-handed game. It should be noted that the Tens composing this quartette must all be in trumps, as no score is permissible for a combination of four assorted Tens.

DECLARING. On winning a trick, a player may either declare or leave the declaration to his partner, with the formula " I leave it to you, partner." The declarer may score a combination, either with his own cards (including the cards already declared by him and lying face upwards on the table), or with one or more of his own cards plus one or more of his partner's declared cards. Thus, if Y and Z are partners, Y is entitled as declarer, if holding the requisite cards, to declare a Sequence by adding Ace, Ten and J to a Royal Marriage he has previously declared ; or if Z has declared the Royal Marriage, by adding his own Ace, Ten and J to Z's Royal Marriage. In the case of Quintuple Bézique (involving, as it does, 10 cards), the declaration *must* involve two or more of partner's declared cards, as the declarer has only nine cards in his hand, and must use up one of these to take the trick.

The other rules dealing with declarations (making of trumps, restoring defective combinations, etc.) are the same as in Rubicon Bézique.

COMPUTATION OF THE SCORE. The procedure here is exactly as in Rubicon Bézique, except that :

(i) The bonus for game is 1,000 (not 500).
(ii) The " Rubicon " is 2,500 (instead of 1,000).
(iii) Brisques (Aces and Tens) are disregarded.

OTHER VARIETIES OF BÉZIQUE

BÉZIQUE WITHOUT A TURN-UP. In this game no card is turned up after dealing; until a Marriage is declared there are no trumps; the first Marriage declared determines trumps; the Seven of trumps has no scoring value—otherwise the game is the same as ordinary Bézique.

TWO-HANDED BÉZIQUE WITH THREE PACKS. In this game, which is played with three packs of Bézique cards, the play is identical with that of ordinary Bézique, except that Triple Bézique counts 1,500.

THREE-HANDED BÉZIQUE. Here, again, three packs of Bézique cards, or 96 cards in all, are used. Each player plays for himself.

Triple Bézique counts 1,500—otherwise the play is the same as in ordinary Bézique.

CRIBBAGE

Of the many "duelling" card games, Cribbage has a fascination peculiarly its own. It calls for sharpness in the perception of possibilities, and for concentration, and it undoubtedly maintains its popularity because of the fact that it is so full of "life" and action.

Cribbage may be played by two, three, or four players, and there are three main variations—Five-card, Six-card and Seven-card Cribbage. In spite of the fact that each of these variations furnishes an excellent opportunity for skill and enjoyment at cards. it can be taken that Five-card Cribbage is the accepted standard and that the two-handed game which, beyond all doubt, is the most scientific, is also the most popular.

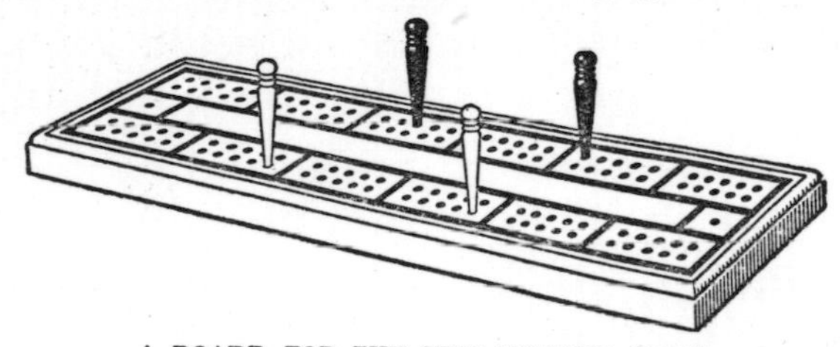

A BOARD FOR THE TWO-HANDED GAME

All varieties of Cribbage are played with the full pack of fifty-two cards, and points are marked on a special "Cribbage board," on either side of the top of which is a double row of thirty holes, each divided into sections of five or—put in another way, sixty holes in tens. At each end in the centre of the board between the two columns, is a "Game" hole. Bone, ivory or wooden pegs—each player having two—are used to mark the scores in the following manner ; if the player's first score be two he places one of his pegs in the second hole of the outer row nearest to him at his "game-hole" end of the board ; should the next score be three he places his second peg three holes ahead of the first, and with each succeeding score the hindmost peg is taken "over" the other and placed the requisite number of holes ahead. When the first line of holes is completed he doubles back along the second, ending always at his own "Game" hole.

A more elaborate form of board is that in which each hole is provided with its own peg, which can be pulled up to indicate the score, the back pegs either being pushed down again or left standing. The board, especially in circles in which pegs are liable to be lost or mislaid, has its advantages—although in many schools there seems to be little objection to replacing a missing peg with the stick of a spent match!

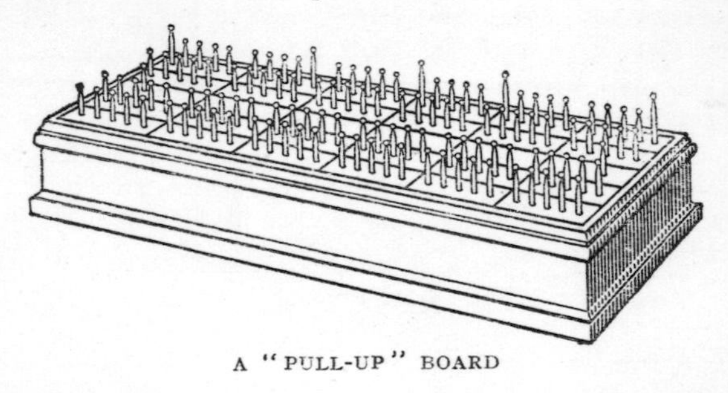

A "PULL-UP" BOARD

The board should always be placed in a central position between the two players.

The object of the game is to form various combinations—Pairs, "Fifteens," Sequences, etc., as explained later—either during the fall of the cards or in the "hand" and "Crib" after the cards have been played. "Game" is sixty-one points in Five-card, one hundred and twenty-one in Six-card, and one hundred and eighty-one in Seven-card Cribbage.

Cards rank as from King high, down through Q, J, 10, 9, 8, etc. to Ace, which is always the lowest. Court cards count as 10s except when used for "pairing," for "pairs" must be of equal rank—Queens for instance, can pair only with each other, and not with a 10, J or K.

Deal is decided by cutting and "low" deals, Ace again counting as one. Either player may shuffle, but the dealer's opponent cuts. In dealing, the cards must be given alternately to each player, beginning with the opponent. The loser of the game deals the next hand.

Misdeals are penalized. Two points are awarded to an opponent for (1) failure to have the pack cut (2) dealing card incorrectly and failing to correct error before dealing the next card (3) exposing a card while dealing, and (4) dealing too many or too few cards to same player. The opponent can demand a re-deal and in the case of either of the first three faults named, may look at his hand before deciding whether or not to exercise this right. If the dealer has an incorrect number of cards the opponent may say whether or not a deal stands even though he has looked at his hand. If the deal stands and the dealer has too many cards, the opponent may draw superfluous cards from the dealer's hand and place them on top of the pack with the added right of looking at them if the dealer has seen them. In the event of the dealer having too few cards, he must supply the deficiency from the top of the pack. If the opponent's hand is short he must decide whether there shall be a re-deal before looking at his hand. Points for misdealing must be claimed and scored immediately. In the event of a card being "faced" in the pack a new deal by the same dealer is compulsory, as also when a pack is found to be "short"; but in this case scores already made with the incorrect pack stand.

THE FIVE CARD GAME. As soon as the deal is complete, each player being given alternately (as mentioned above) five cards, each player looks at his cards and throws out, face downwards, two of them which go to form what is always referred to as the "Crib." As there is a slight advantage in the first deal of each separate game the non-dealer is allowed to score at once "Three for Last."

After the Crib—which is the property of the dealer—has been thrown out the non-dealer again cuts the cards, and the dealer turns the top card of the remainder of the pack, shows it, and replaces it face up on top of the undealt cards. This faced card is known as the " Start " and belongs for scoring purposes to both players; should it be a Knave the dealer scores immediately two points, described as " Two for his Heels," but it must be scored before the dealer plays his first card, otherwise the right is forfeited. The game is now open and the non-dealer starts the play by leading a card, to which his opponent replies.

Before describing an actual game of Cribbage, perhaps it will be as well if we give the system of scoring which, as has been mentioned above, can be divided into two branches, viz. (1) that which takes place during the play of the hand, and (2) that which takes place when the play is over.

(1) During the play of the hand a player making a Pair—i.e., playing a card of the same value as the last one played—scores two; if he makes a Pair-Royal—by playing a third card of the same value to two already played—he scores six; and for a Double Pair-Royal (i.e., a fourth card added to the Pair-Royal), twelve. For making Fifteen or Thirty-one, i.e., playing a card which makes a total of either of those numbers when added to those already exposed (omitting the Start), two are scored. An important position arises out of the Thirty-one count. If the cards on the table are approaching this total and the next player cannot play without passing it he must call " Go." The other player can then play any other card or cards of his hand up to the limit. If they make Thirty-one exactly he scores two, and if not he scores only one—which is described as " For the Last Card." The hand is then terminated and the players proceed to the " Show."

Sequences are also scored during the play of the hand—one point for each card in a run of three or more, suits being disregarded. They need not be played in regular order, so long as the cards exposed at any one time form an unbroken series. The player of the third card in sequence scores his three points even though the cards come out, say, as 5-7-6. Then if a fourth card adding to the sequence is played—in this case a 4 or an 8—the player putting down this fourth card scores four points, and so on. The limit of a Sequence is seven. Ace counts only as one for this as for other purposes in Cribbage; thus Ace, 2, 3 is a Sequence, Q, K, Ace is not. An intervening card breaks the Sequence, as also a pair. It should be noted that although in the scoring all Aces and Court cards count ten, in making Sequences, Pairs, etc., they retain the order of their face value.

(2). After the cards have been played out and the scores arising out of the course of play have been duly pegged, each player proceeds to count all possible points in his hand, taking up again all his cards for this purpose and bringing in the "Start." The non-dealer commences, scoring as he makes his points, then the dealer counts first the score in his hand, and then goes on to count all points in his "Crib," also combined with the "Start." Here it should be noted that "Flushes" have scoring value, three points being taken for a hand containing three cards (not reckoning the Start) of a suit, and four when the Start also is of the same suit. If a hand contains a Knave of the same suit as the Start the holder can score "One for his Nob."

In counting for Crib, points are made in exactly the same way as in the hand, with the exception that a Flush cannot be scored unless the Start card is of the same suit as the rest, when five points are taken. The following summary shows at a glance all the scores that can be made in Hand and Crib.

SCORES MADE IN COURSE OF PLAY

Pair	2 points
Pair-Royal (Threes or Triplets)... ...	6 ,,
Double Pair-Royal (Fours)	12 ,,
Sequence of Three	3 ,,
For each additional card in sequence ...	1 ,,
Fifteen	2 ,,
Thirty-one	2 ,,
"Go"	1 ,,
Last Card	1 ,,
Last Card combined with Fifteen ...	3 ,,
For "His Heels"	2 ,,
To non-dealer (1st deal only)	3 ,,

SCORES MADE IN HAND AND CRIB. Here the Start is reckoned as belonging to both the Hands and the Crib, consequently larger and rather more complicated scores are the rule :

For Pairs, Pair-Royals, Double Pair-Royals, Sequences, and Fifteens	as above
For a Flush of 3, in Hand only... ...	3 points
For a Flush of 4, in Hand with Start ...	4 ,,
For a Flush of 5, in Crib with Start ...	5 ,,
For "His Nob"	1 ,,

Before proceeding to demonstrate how a game works out in detail we can now discuss with good purpose one or two important pointers in policy play. First, as to which are the best cards to be thrown out for Crib.

As the Crib belongs to the dealer he should take pains to throw out those cards that are likely to increase its value and, bearing the possibility of "Fifteens" in mind, he will probably first remember that there are in the pack many more "tens" than any other value, so will, perhaps, throw out a pair of 5s if he has them, though in doing so he will realize that he is to some extent lessening his chances of scoring Fifteens in the play. His two 5s in the Crib will make one pair a certainty, and there is always the chance of catching one or more 10s ; or he might himself throw out a 5 and a 10, thus making one Fifteen a certainty. Two cards of the same suit will give the possibility of a "Flush" ; cards of identical value are good also as they form a pair to start with, and if the opponent happens to throw out a similar card, will make up a Pair-Royal. Sequence cards as throw-outs may also prove beneficial, as they may be joined by a third that will continue the series ; and the same with an 8 and a 7 (which already form a Fifteen), for these have good prospects of resulting in a Sequence. If you cannot (without damaging your hand), discard a Pair, a Fifteen, or a run ; two alternate cards—a 5 and a 7, for instance—are better than widely separated cards, for there is always the chance of the wanted Sequence card joining them. In discarding, the non-dealer will, of course, " go opposite " to this principle and will do his best to baulk the Crib. He must throw out cards that are least likely to help the Crib-holder and will therefore avoid where possible putting out the type of cards and combinations indicated as being best for the dealer.

After a little practice with one who knows the game the novice will soon find that, in spite of the fact that the points seem ridiculously small when compared with those awarded to, say, the successful Contract player, high scores are possible from a few cards, and that Cribbage can be quite as exciting as any other Card game. Take, for instance, a Crib containing four 5's and a 10 (admittedly a very rare occurrence).

THE HIGHEST POSSIBLE ONE-HAND SCORE

Here there are six Pairs for twelve and eight Fifteens for sixteen, twenty-eight in all; while if the 10 happens to be a Knave of the same suit as the Start (but not the Start itself), it is twenty-nine, the highest score possible at Cribbage. Again, in a hand of four of a kind you may have a Double Pair-Royal, counting twelve; while if the four cards happen to be 5's you have four Fifteens (eight) in addition, making the score twenty. In a Crib of, say, four 7's and an Ace the score would be twelve for a Double Pair-Royal and twelve for six Fifteens, making twenty-four in all. Note that to count Pairs when holding more than one (without missing any) a simple method is to place the three cards of equal value in a triangle and remember that each side makes a pair—a score of six. When four pairing cards are held, set them out in a square and take two for each side and two for each diagonal, the total thus being twelve.

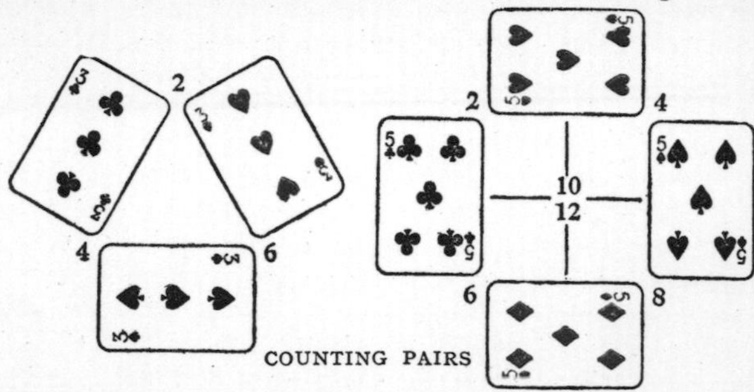

COUNTING PAIRS

The number of combinations that may be held at Cribbage are, of course, legion; and, while it would serve no useful purpose to go into them exhaustively, we feel that a list of a few of the more confusing would be of benefit to the student. One "Fifteen" is scored as Fifteen-two; two Fifteens as Fifteen-four and so on. Here, then, are the scores of some Hands in the Five-card game:

5 and three 10s in sequence (Fifteen-six and a run of three) 9

6, 6, 7, 8 (Fifteen-two, Pair four and double run of three) 10

5, 5, 10, J (or other court card) 10

5, 5, 10, 10 (or other pair of 10s) ... 12

6, 6, 9, 9 (Fifteen-eight and two pairs) ... 12

3, 3, 3, 9
3, 6, 6, 6
6, 6, 6, 9
6, 9, 9, 9
7, 7, 7, A
7, 7, 7, 8
7, 8, 8, 8 } (each scoring Fifteen-six and a Pair-Royal) 12

4, 4, 5, 6
4, 5, 5, 6
4, 5, 6, 6 } (Fifteen-four, Pair six, and double run of three) 12

5, 5, 5, 10 (Fifteen-eight and a Pair-Royal) 14

5, 5, 5, 5 (Fifteen-eight and a double Pair-Royal) 20

In the Crib—as in the Hand at Six-card Cribbage—the extra card very largely increases the possible number of combinations; the following list, therefore, merely gives a selection of some of the higher scores, and in it "N" indicates "His Nob" and "S" the Start:

Cards	Score
5, 5, 5, 5, 10	28
7, 7, 8, 8, 9	24
7, 7, 7, 7, 1	24
4, 5, 5, 6, 6	24
4, 4, 4, 4, 7	24
3, 3, 3, 3, 9	24
3, 6, 6, 6, 6	24
5, 5, J, N, 5, S	23
5, 5, 5, 4, 6	23
5, 5, 5, 10, 10	22
4, 5, 6, 6, 6	21
7, 7, 7, 8, 9	21
3, 3, 3, 4, 5	21
3, 4, 4, 4, 4	20
3, 3, 6, 6, 6	20
3, 3, 4, 4, 5	20
6, 6, 7, 7, 8	20
6, 6, 9, 9, 9	20
7, 7, 7, 8, 8	20
7, 8, 8, 9, 9	20
7, 7, 7, A, A	20

(Note that 19 is an impossible score).

Cards	Score
5, 5, 10, N, Q	18
3, 3, 3, 6, 6	18
5, 5, J, Q, K	17
2, 3, 4, 4, 4	17
A, A, 2, 2, 3	16
2, 2, 3, 3, 4	16
2, 6, 7, 7, 8	16
6, 7, 8, 9, 9	16

When "Game" is reached another scoring factor may arise. If a winner reaches "Game" before his opponent has gone half-way (i.e., scored Thirty-one in the Five-card game) a "Lurch" is scored, i.e., the winner scores two games instead of one. Another "extra" counting occurs when a player fails to peg the full value of his cards, either in play or otherwise. His opponent must at once proclaim him as "Muggins," point out the omission, and promptly score the neglected points on his own side of the board.

And now let us play through a specimen game to demonstrate the run and the methods of scoring as it proceeds. If this game is studied and carefully played over, several of the fine points that lend to Cribbage its chief fascination will be more thoroughly appreciated.

The two players are Mr. X and Mr. Y, and Mr. Y is dealing. The first hands dealt come as follows:

X holds—♠ Ace, J, 6; ♦ 5; ♣ 5
Y (dealer)—♠ 5, 7, 8; ♦ Ace; ♥ 5

Suppose that X throws out for Crib the 6 and Ace of Spades, and Y the 7 and 8 of the same suit, the hands held by each will now stand as follows:

X—♠ J; ♦ 5; ♣ 5
Y—♠ 5; ♥ 5; ♦ Ace

X cuts to Y, and 9 of Spades is turned up by way of Start.

X leads his J of Spades, to which Y plays his 5 of Hearts—making Fifteen. He promptly calls "Fifteen-two" and pegs two accordingly. X next plays the 5 of Diamonds—calling "twenty" (the new total) and scores two for a Pair; on which Y plays the 5 of Spades, calling "twenty-five," and scoring six for a Pair-Royal. X now plays the 5 of Clubs, calling "thirty" and scoring twelve for a Double Pair-Royal; whereupon Y throws his last card, the Ace of Diamonds, calls "thirty-one," and scores two for completing that number.

X has thus scored in play, as it is termed, 14, and Y 10; but it remains to be seen what they can score by their cards, this being, as explained above, a separate operation. X, as non-dealer, has "first show." Each of his 5s combine with the J to form Fifteen, which he claims by saying "Fifteen-two, Fifteen-four." The two 5s form a Pair two more) and the J being of the same suit as the Turn-up card, he scores one additional point—"One for his Nob"—for this; in all seven points.

Y has Fifteen-four, for each of his 5s combines with his A, and the 9 of Spades, the Start (which as we have before stated, is counted with each player's hand); and he also scores two for his pair of 5s. The Crib also belongs to Y, as dealer, and here he is more fortunate, for it consists of the Ace, 6, 7, 8 of Spades, and the Start is the 9 of the same suit. Now, 7 and 8 make Fifteen, likewise both Ace, 6, 8 and 6, 9. Y counts accordingly for these, Fifteen-two, Fifteen-four, Fifteen-six. But he has also four cards (6,7,8,9) in *Sequence*, and for these he is entitled to four points. Furthermore, all the cards, both Crib and Turn-up, are of *the same suit*, and he accordingly marks five (one for each card) for a Flush. As we have seen, a Flush can be scored in the Crib only when the Turn-up is of the same suit as the rest; in the hand of either player this is not necessary.

Now let us play the next hand, X dealing, and illustrate some further points. When the cards are picked up the hands are as follows:

Y holds—♥ J, 7; ♠ 7; ♦ 6; ♣ 3
X holds—♥ Ace, K, 5; ♦ 8; ♣ 9

Y begins by throwing out for Crib the J of Hearts and 3 of Clubs, and X the K and 5 of Hearts, leaving the playing hands thus:

Y—♥ 7; ♠ 7; ♦ 6
X—♥ Ace; ♦ 8; ♣ 9

X turns up the J of Diamonds, scoring "Two for his Heels" accordingly.

Y now leads the 7 of Hearts, in the hope that X may make a pair, when he would cap it with a Pair-Royal; but X returns the 8 of Diamonds, calling "Fifteen," and scoring two points. To this Y plays the 6 of Diamonds, calling "twenty-one" and scoring three for Sequence (6,7,8); and X plays the 9 of Clubs, calling "thirty," and scoring four for the new Sequence (6, 7, 8, 9). Y has no answer to make to this, for he cannot play without over-passing the limit—thirty-one, so says "Go," and X at once plays his Ace of Hearts, calling "Thirty-one," and scoring two points. In most schools play is now over, but in some Y plays his one remaining card and pegs one for "last card."

Y has now "first show," but can only score a Pair (the two 7s), the Start being here of no advantage to him. Had it chanced to be an 8, it would have increased the value of his hand to twelve, viz., Fifteen-four (each of the 7s combining with the 8), two Sequences of three each (6, 7, 8 twice over), and a pair for the two 7s. X has not a single point. The Turn-up card has not helped him beyond the "Two for his Heels" already taken. Had it been a 10 he would have scored three for a Sequence (8, 9, 10) or had it been a 7 he would likewise have scored three for a Sequence, and two for a Fifteen (7 and 8) in addition.

But X has yet to take the Crib, consisting of the K, J, 5 of Hearts and 3 of Clubs. The last mentioned card does not affect the result, but the 5 combines with the two other cards and with the Start (J of Diamonds) to produce three Fifteens—scored as "Fifteen-six"—and the J of Hearts combines with the J of Diamonds to form a Pair—an additional two points.

Each player deals alternately until the one or the other has scored sixty-one points, when the game is at an end.

CRIBBAGE VARIATIONS

Six and Seven-Card Cribbage. In these varieties of the game, except for the fact that in the one case six, and in the other seven, cards are dealt to each player, there is no difference in the play—or in the Crib—and very little in the procedure. Indeed, the only real differences are that the non-dealer does not take his three extra points for "last," and that all the cards are played out to the end, the player failing to score for the "Go" leading again, thus giving his opponent the chance of making a Pair or Fifteen.

In both varieties scores are piled up with much greater rapidity than in the ordinary Five-card game; it is, therefore, usual in the Six-card game to play twice round the board (one hundred and twenty-one points) and in the Seven-card game three times (one hundred and eighty-one points).

Three-Handed Cribbage. This is a game for three players, and for it special scoring-boards are constructed. In some forms the board is a hollow triangle with the peg-holes placed on each of the three limbs, in another an extra limb can be swung out on a pivot from the ordinary board; this type is illustrated on p. 115.

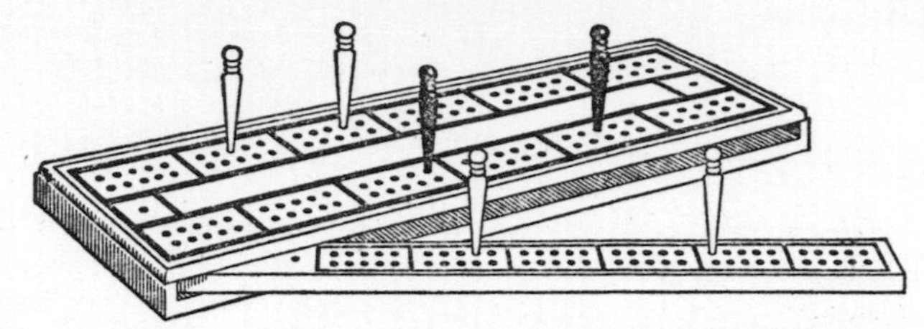

A FORM OF BOARD FOR THE THREE-HANDED GAME

Five cards are dealt to each player, and an extra one to the Crib, to which each player contributes one card only. The player to the left of the dealer leads, has "first show" and deals in the succeeding hand. Again, there are no "three points for last" for non-dealer, but otherwise play and procedure are exactly as in the ordinary game. It is left to the particular "school" to decide—before play commences—whether sixty-one or one hundred and twenty-one points shall be the objective.

FOUR-HANDED CRIBBAGE. In this variety two play against two as partners, each side taking opposite sides of the table. Partners are usually arranged Whist fashion, i.e., by cutting—the two highest against the two lowest, and lowest having first deal. Each player is dealt five cards, and each throws one out to form the Crib which—as in all Cribbage games—is the property of the dealer. Consultation between players, and suggestions by one partner to another, are alike prohibited, but there is no objection to a player helping his partner in the count of hand or Crib. The hand is played out as in the Six-card game—there is no stopping just because Thirty-one is reached, but otherwise, play and procedure is as in the Five-card game described above, Game usually being one hundred and twenty-one points.

POKER

THE origin of Poker—like that of so many other good things—is obscure. Some say that it is a direct descendant of *Poque*, an old French game in which bluffing seems to have played a considerable part; others that it had its birth in the American backwoods of early days, whence, undoubtedly, its many refinements and variations have sprung. This may or may not be the case—but although Poker is to-day almost as popular in England as in the United States, it is still in the unhappy position of having no official Code of Laws, and it seems a pity that some recognized authority—the Portland Club or the Whist Club of New York, for instance—does not take it under its wing and for all time silence argument by drawing up and promulgating a set of Rules and Regulations. In the absence of such, however, we will attempt here to describe and codify the game as it is usually played in the leading clubs.

Two outstanding features combine to make Poker a popular and social game. First, almost any number of players from two to eight can take part in it, and while play is in progress conversation can proceed at will; and, second, each player stands on his own—he has no partner to consider. If he loses he has only himself to blame—or pity. To say that Poker is a gambling game pure and simple is unjustifiable. Speculation predominates, certainly, but, while play does not bring on brain-fag, as may a long spell at Contract or Chess, the mind is constantly at work studying possibilities and the mannerisms of one's opponents. To be successful one must be a student of psychology and must at times refrain from betting, even when one has a good hand. Quick thinking is essential; and, above all, one who wishes to excel at the game should cultivate the " poker " face, by which we mean, obtain such control over the feelings and the excitement of the moment that no change of expression, involuntary movement, or gesture, will ever betray what is going on in one's mind and, possibly, reflect the nature of the hand.

Poker is played with the ordinary pack of 52 cards, either with or without the "Joker" (see p. 130), though in some "schools" when there are only 3 or 4 players the 2s and 3s are removed, and when there are more than seven taking part the special 60-card pack, containing two additional cards (11- and 12-spot) in each suit, is used. The cards rank from Ace down to 3, 2, the Ace always counting high, except that in sequence it may be either high or low (forming sequence of Ace, 2, 3, 4, 5 or 10, J, Q, K, Ace).

The object of each player is to hold the highest of the various possible combinations of 5 cards (see p. 125) that are in play during any particular hand. In "Straight Poker" the original game from which all the numerous variations are derived, these had to be held in the cards as dealt; in "Draw Poker," the more usual form nowadays and, consequently, that which we proceed to describe, all have the opportunity of discarding and filling up from the undealt stock. The highest hand in the final show takes whatever happens to be in the pool.

Draw Poker

The dealer having been selected, and the shuffling and cutting effected in the usual way, the cards are dealt (one at a time from left to right), until each player has five, the last, of course, falling to the dealer, and the deal passing in rotation to the left.

Preceding the deal there are three little points that should be settled. As we have hinted above, there is gambling in Poker (indeed, it may be said at once that it is one of those games which simply can't be played for "love")—so before the start the company should arrange among themselves (1) the amount of the "Ante" (2) the limit to which the bets may be raised, and (3) the time at which play should end.

The "Ante" is the amount put into the Pool by the

"Age" (i.e., the player on the immediate left of the dealer) before the cards are dealt (hence also known, in his case, as the "blind"), the same amount at least being put in in rotation by each member of the party who, after looking at his cards, decides to come in. It is open to the age to double the ante ("straddle") if he wishes to do so; if he does each succeeding player must put in the new amount, unless the player next to him also straddles, in which case the twice-doubled amount is subscribed by each, dealer—if he decides to come in after looking at his cards—making up his blind to the requisite amount. Any player may straddle provided that he sits next either to the dealer or to a previous straddler.

Nowadays Clubs frequently take it upon themselves to fix limits, and incidentally, in many cases, provide a room exclusively for Pokerites, no mere spectators being allowed to enter. But as our exposition is intended to interest and be a guidance to the family circle as well as to clubmen, we will for the purpose of argument fix the stake at £1, with 2s. rises (or less, but not coppers),—and 5s. ante money. In other words, before the draw, betting can proceed in shilling stages up to 5s. (the limit), and after the draw in 2s. stages up to £1 (the limit). Thus if there are six players at the table and they all bet to the limit—a most rare happening—the winner after the show of hands scoops in a Pool worth £7 10s. 0d., plus 3s. as penalty from each opponent if the winning hand happens to be a Royal Flush (see p. 125). So, on this selected scale, a player, venturing to the limit, is liable to lose £1 5s. 0d. in a round, leaving out the Royal Flush penalty. Counters are invariably substituted for coins at the table in Clubs (a banker being appointed for exchange) but we purposely refer to the coins of the realm, as "money talks" more convincingly, better conveying what can be lost or won during a flutter—though it may be mentioned that in actual play some are inclined to be more reckless with counters or chips than with legal tender!

The propriety of making limits of some kind is obvious, for in their absence he with the longest purse must inevitably empty the purses of all the others; the time limit is also of importance, as very little experience of the game will show.

Probably the ideal school at Poker is a party of six, more than seven is inclined to be confusing and unwieldy; but one of the chief charms of the game is that—within limits—the numbers taking part may be indefinite, for in between hands anybody may drop out or come in. You can leave the table at your will; it is not incumbent upon you to run the risk of failing to keep an appointment, a danger which a protracted game of Contract or Auction Bridge might entail.

The Dealer temporarily presides over the proceedings; he gives a ruling as to any alleged breach of regulations that may possibly arise, and is expected to see that everything is in order. The player on his immediate right (the "Pone"), has the privilege of cutting the pack after it has been shuffled; and the player on his immediate left (the "Age" or "Ante-man") is, as we have seen, the only one who pays into the Pool before the Deal commences, and it is the duty of the Dealer to see that this is done. As we have selected £1 as the maximum stake for betting, the Age's opening contribution is one shilling.

During the deal, if the Dealer should turn a card face upwards by accident, that card must be accepted by the player, who can, however, claim a fresh deal if a second card is exposed in his hand. If a player exposes any or all of his own cards he has no remedy—he can either play on or throw in, and in the latter event forfeits whatever he has deposited. When a player receives too few (or too many) cards and calls attention to the fact before seeing any card, he can, prior to any betting, demand a fresh deal. Alternatively, if the Dealer permits, he can have a card withdrawn when there is one too many, or be supplied with another to complete the five. In the case of one too many in a hand, the Dealer does not throw it away, but places it at the bottom of the pack, unseen. If the Dealer gives two cards in place of one to a player, he may rectify the mistake by passing the under card on to the next player ; if he deals out one hand short, it is a mis-deal.

Always count your cards before turning them, for it is fatal if you discover after seeing any of your cards that you have one too many. Then you have no option but to throw it in, and lose your stake—if any. In case of a player finding on looking at his cards that he has only four, he can remain in if he chooses and make up for the deficiency during the subsequent draw. Finally, if in the course of dealing, the back of a card be found with a "foreign" mark, the pack must be cast aside and a fresh one substituted. A deal out of turn must be stopped before it is completed, or it stands. No player who has glanced at his cards can claim a new deal for any reason, but for that of an imperfect pack.

The deal completed, each player picks up his hand of five cards and mentally weighs up its possibilities, separating the "wheat from the chaff." As already mentioned, the Age has, prior to the start of the deal, put up his ante money—a shilling. The player next him on the left must put up the same amount if he wants to draw cards to improve his hand. Perhaps he has all the "chaff" and no "wheat," so he throws his cards into the centre of the table. If he comes in, he can cover the ante money or straddle, making 2s. in all. The next player, if he plays, puts down 2s. or if he likes he can again straddle (putting in 4s.), while the next player (only) has the option of raising the contribution to 5s., our agreed limit for the ante money. The remaining players (say six in all) declare in rotation whether they remain in or not. Those who do stand their ground have to put 5s. (or whatever limit has been put up) in the pool, and the Age, if he decides likewise, has to cover his "blind" with another 4s. or lose it.

When all who are coming in have put up equal amounts in the pool, the Dealer picks up the stock and asks the player nearest him on the left how many cards he wishes, and so on in rotation. Each player when asked *(and not before)*, may discard as many of his five cards as he chooses or, if he prefers, he may stand "pat" (i.e., keep his original five cards)—"throw outs" are deposited in the centre of the table, face down. Every player must announce distinctly the number of cards he wants, so that all at the table can hear. Why this is essential the novice will soon realise; it may (or may not) be valuable information, showing strength or weakness, and very possibly affecting subsequent draws. Even the Dealer must state (when he asks himself "How many") how many cards he draws. After the work of discarding has been entirely completed, no one is allowed, however, to ask, or to mention, how many cards were drawn by any particular player; if the question should be put there is no penalty, but it is quite within the rights of the examined party to refuse the information.

Harking back to the commencement of the discarding: the Dealer's pack in hand must not be shuffled or cut again, and the additional cards must be distributed, one by one, from the top. If any card is found "faced" in the pack at this stage, it is deposited with the discards. Should a card be accidentally faced by the Dealer, it cannot be replaced until all the other players, including the Dealer himself, have been handed their desired number of cards.

A card thrown among the discards cannot be returned to a hand under any circumstances. If a player asks for too few or too many cards, and they are placed before him by the Dealer, the mistake may be rectified should he discover it before he has glanced at any of them and before the next player has been served, otherwise (if he has asked for too many) he must discard so as to keep them, a proceeding that may mean destroying a Pair or Threes, or any other combination he had in view. If he eventually discovers (after he has drawn) that he has only four cards, he can remain in, but if he finds he has more than five, he has to throw in at once, sacrificing whatever he has previously staked. If the Dealer hands himself too many cards he must take them. If a player allows another on his left to draw cards out of his proper turn, the wrongdoer is not penalized, but the other is—

for neglecting to apply at the proper time. He must either play his hand without drawing, or abandon it. It may be that in the course of the passage of a card from the Dealer to a player, the latter has caught sight of it—an instance of careless or slovenly dealing. The player for whom the card was intended can, if he chooses, state that he has sighted it, declare its denomination, and have another, but not until after the other players have drawn. Should he be mistaken in his declaration he has to retain his original card.

When there are more than six players, it may happen that there are not sufficient cards to go round; in this case the last card must not be handed out, but be placed by the Dealer among the discards and abandoned hands, which are then gathered together by him, shuffled, and cut by the Pone. The Dealer then completes the work of "filling up" hands by using them as a new stock. In parenthesis—those who have been kept waiting to be replenished must retain their throw-outs until asked how many they require. It is obvious that if discards are placed among those cards that have been requisitioned in the shuffle, there is a danger of one or more of one's own throw-outs finding their way back.

We should mention here, that, as a point of etiquette, it is highly unsporting for a player who has thrown in his hand and become, temporarily or otherwise, a spectator, to overlook other players' hands—unless, of course, invited to do so. In this way one may glean valuable information for future guidance, learning, for instance (without paying for it), that a particular party is fond of drawing two cards when he has only a pair, of keeping a "kicker," or that he places an unusually high value on his cards. In fact, many valuable inferences may be drawn through peeping at other players' hands.

It is now time to explain just what the object of the game is; we have already mentioned, in brief, that it is to hold the highest of the various combinations, but we have not said what they are. There are ten of them, and we give them here in their relative order of value, beginning at the lowest:

(1) Five Odd Cards that bear no relation to each other, such as Q of Spades, J of Clubs, 9 of Diamonds, 6 of Clubs and 3 of Hearts. This is an almost worthless collection, and yet there are times when it is the best hand out, for in a show against a similar set the highest card in either hand wins. This hand would be declared as "Queen High," and could be beaten by a "King High" or "Ace High." Almost invariably such hands are "thrown in."

(2) A Pair—i.e., two cards of the the same pip-value, say a pair of Sevens of any suit and three other cards. Ordinarily the three outsiders are discarded, but some players prefer to retain the Ace as a "Kicker" (a worthless but high card kept in the hope of getting a similar one), or with the idea of deceiving opponents. There are three possible developments in drawing to a pair. The two Sevens may finish as three, or even four Sevens, or may be turned into a "Full Hand"—(see p. 124, para. 7).

(3) Two Pairs—e.g., two Jacks and two Eights. In this case the fifth card is generally thrown in, and if the replacement happens to be another J or Eight, the holder has a "full hand." That is the only possible way of improving, hence many players are not keen on being "born" with "Two Pair." The odds against them filling the "Full Hand" are so great that on occasions they are prompted to stand "pat" in the hope of leading opponents to believe that it is a hand that cannot be improved—as a "Straight," "Flush," or "Full Hand."

(4) Threes—i.e., three cards of the same pip-value—three Kings, Queens, Jacks, Tens, etc. The remaining two are discarded in the hope of securing "Fours" or a "Full Hand." It has been mathematically worked out that it is more difficult to improve on Threes than on Two Pair, but a lot of seasoned Pokerites are difficult to convince on this point.

(5) A Straight—i.e., a hand containing all five cards in proper sequence, but of mixed denomination—say, Ten of Clubs, Nine of Hearts, Eight of Spades, Seven of Diamonds, and Six of Diamonds. Of course

if you are dealt with this you stand "pat." Should you originally have the first four cards, and the Five of Diamonds instead of the Six, you throw in the latter. You may pick up a six or a Jack, either of which would give you the sequence. In Straights, the Ace, as we have seen, plays a double rôle. A Straight hand of five, four, three, two and Ace is declared as "Five High," and a Straight consisting of Ace, King, Queen, Jack, Ten is declared "Ace High." If two players hold Straights, the highest value card decides the winner; when two or more are of equal value, the pool must be divided.

(6) A FLUSH—i.e., five cards of the same suit. When two flushes are shown against each other, the winning combination is the one that contains the highest card or cards. In a Flush, the Ace always counts highest, so a hand formed of Ace, Two, Three, Four and Eight would beat a Flush with a King High, whatever the other cards. If in the deal you have four Diamonds and a Heart, you throw in the latter, hoping to draw another Diamond; should you fail the hand is worthless—though even then you may, by a bold bluff, frighten away the opposition.

"FULL HOUSE"

(7) FULL HAND—i.e., a Pair and a Three. If there is more than one Full Hand shown, the tie is decided by the highest Three. Thus three Sixes and a pair of Aces are inferior to three Sevens and a pair of Twos. The unbeatable Full Hand ("Full House" some term it) is three Aces along with any kind of Pair. No two Full Hands can be of equal value, so there can be no division of the Pool.

(8) FOURS—i.e., four cards of the same denomination; four Tens, for instance. The fifth card is of no consequence as—unless the Joker (see p. 130) is in use—the Hand cannot be improved. Yet the worthless one is invariably discarded solely with the idea of mystifying the opposition. They might conclude you are drawing to Two Pair, Straight, or Flush, and the last thing they would think was that you were born with Fours, so rarely does it happen. Only when you start wagering will you make the opposition sit up and take notice! It is hardly probable that you will find yourself confronted by another hand of Fours—it is millions to one against such a possibility. With "pat" Fours the wagering prospect is better than the player who comes in with Threes and fills Fours, for then the opponents deduce that he starts with Threes, but when one card is drawn, the opponents are kept wondering what is the actual objective. Of course there are times—but they are few and far between—when a Pair develops into Fours, and then the lucky holder is on velvet.

(9) STRAIGHT FLUSH—i.e., a Straight and Flush combined—a sequence all of the same suit. There is no difference in value or rank as far as suits are concerned.

(10) ROYAL FLUSH—this is the last and best of the possible combinations, a glorified Straight Flush, viz., the Ace, King, Queen, Jack and Ten of a suit; it cannot be beaten. So rarely does the combination turn up that the holder, in addition to scooping up the money in the pool, draws a certain amount (in proportion to the stake prevailing throughout the game) from each player at the table. It is called "penalty money," and in most clubs it is the practice that when this most rare event happens, the Royal Flush holder stands a round of refreshment—as, in golf clubs, a member is expected to celebrate his performance of "holing in one" by hospitality to all members at the "nineteenth" hole.

The relative value of the preceding ten combinations has been decided by the mathematical chances of the

Deal and the rarest combination naturally ranks the highest. The odds against receiving in a Deal any of these combinations have been calculated as follows :

Hand	Odds Against	Number in all possible combinations
One Pair	1¼ to 1 ...	1,098,240
Two Pair	20 to 1 ...	123,552
Threes	46 to 1 ...	54,912
Sequence	254 to 1 ...	10,200
Flush	508 to 1 ...	5,100
Full Hand ...	693 to 1 ...	3,744
Fours	4,164 to 1 ...	624
Straight Flush ...	72,192 to 1 ...	26
Royal Flush ...	649,739 to 1 ...	4

There are 2,598,960 different combinations of five cards possible in the pack (excluding Joker) ; 1,302,540 hold no Pair, Sequence or Flush.

The chances are 2½ to 1 against improving a Pair by drawing three cards ; 8 to 1 against making Threes or Two Pair ; 61 to 1 against a Full Hand ; 364 to 1 against Fours ; 4 to 1 against improving a Pair by drawing two cards ; 8 to 1 against Two Pair ; and 12 to 1 against Threes.

They are 12 to 1 against improving a Full Hand by drawing to Two Pair ; 8 to 1 against improving Threes by drawing two ; 14½ to 1 against a Full Hand and 23 to 1 against Fours.

The draw completed, betting follows, and it is opened by the next player to the left of the Age, even if the latter has already retired. It is not incumbent on him to bet—he may have come in originally in the hope of filling a Straight or Flush and failed to fill ; his hand is thus worthless, and so, if he doesn't feel like bluffing, he throws in. Then the next player in turn to the left must decide, and so on. If no one bets, the Age, if he is left in (as is invariably the case), takes the pool. If any player bets, each in turn to the left must see the bet or raise it, or drop out, If, as in the game we have already mentioned, the maximum limit for betting is £1, then the raises must be 2s. a time.

To illustrate how this works out; suppose A (the Age), B, C and D become engaged in a battle royal, each holding a powerful combination, the remaining players having been frightened out. B starts the ball rolling with 2s.; C raises 2s. (4s. in all); D "sees" (i.e., he remains in the betting but does not raise the stake); A raises another 2s.; B does ditto (8s. in all); C raises again (10s. in all); D drops out ("frozen out"—considers the pace too hot for his holding—and forfeits his 4s.); the other three, A, B and C fight to the finish, the closure being applied when they have each staked 20s. reached by advances (raises) of 2s. at a time. The show of hands follows and the player holding the best combination collects the pool. This is an exceptional instance of spirited play, going to the limit, and if an average of half that amount is speculated on each round, the play is highly entertaining—especially to the winners!

Any player who sees or raises out of his turn cannot withdraw his money—money once placed in the pool cannot be taken out of it, except as winnings. When betting is closed, all hands in the call must be shown on the table. A player who is in a call, whether he called the last bet, or his bet was called, must not admit he is beaten and conceal his hand. If the last bet made is not seen, the player takes the pool without being called upon to show his hand. It is, however, allowable for two players who are betting only against each other to agree to divide the pool, but even in this case, their cards must be exposed to the table.

One of the secrets of success at Poker is to know when and how to bet, by calling or raising, so that when a good hand comes one's way, tactics most likely to be productive will be adopted. A common practice with some players is, at the start, to launch on an "advertising campaign," that is, bet on insignificant hands. They maintain that if after a spell of bluffing tactics, they "get the goods," they will then get full value for them.

The player next to the Age is in a wrong position to give signs of strength straight away, and lies low in the hope of seeing possible raises and, if possible, raising further. The Age man is generally looked upon as the most advantageously placed, hence the reason for his deposit of a Blind stake. Often, when he is in the act of completing the first round of betting, he has summed up the situation and can act accordingly. On the other hand, the Age, unless he has the reputation of being an out-and-out stonewaller, is never given credit for holding anything. If he has a high Pair, it is, therefore, good tactics for him to raise, if that has not already been done by others.

An invaluable aid to successful wagering is to keep ever in mind the idiosyncrasies of one's opponents. Don't be given to excessive seeing—it's an impoverishing form of inquisitiveness! The adept Pokerite is ever changing in his methods—thereby confounding the enemy, while the too cautious player (he who is never known to bluff), never gets good value for a good hand, and never, unless he has an extraordinary run of good cards, rises from the table a substantial winner.

It is impossible to estimate the value of a hand. The heaviest losses may be made on Fours. Never think how much you may win on a good hand, but how much you can lose. That is not cowardice ; it is good judgement.

It is reckoned that the player who most frequently holds Two Pairs will win in the end. It is not the pools, (few and far between) which help your pile, but the bulk of the small ones. Sometimes a player has a long spell of miserable hands. He must now exercise patience and only look on till the period of Threes or even better arrives. Then is the time to play them for all they're worth—the time to " push your luck " !

There are some players who make a practice of " cutting their losses." They are prepared to lose £5 and nothing more. On the other hand they remain at the table as long as they are winning. This may be called a selfish attitude, but then—and it's as well to know this—no mercy is given or expected at the Poker table.

VARIATIONS

There are a dozen or more variations to this fascinating game of Poker, all of them hailing from America, and all agreeing with the general principles of comparative value of the cards and hands, the method of dealing, etc., as previously laid down for "Draw Poker." Some of them are merely additional calls, the adoption of which may or may not be agreed upon by the players at the start; others introduce variations in the play and the betting. We will deal with the first-named group first.

"Tiger," "Blaze," "The Skip" and "Round the Corner" are optional and additional combinations. By some they are classed as fantastic, and by none are they reckoned in the general run of play unless the inclusion of one or more has been decided upon before the commencement of play. The ten combinations previously defined are those in universal use.

TIGER is a hand consisting of Seven high and Two low that is devoid of a Pair, Sequence or Flush—in other words, a broken Straight. In order of value it is sandwiched between the ordinary Straight and the Flush.

A BLAZE is five court cards (a "picture gallery") irrespective of rank, with the Ace excluded. Really, a Blaze is only a technical term, as it either forms a Pair, Two Pair or a Full Hand; it ranks between Two Pair and Threes.

A SKIP (also known as a "Dutch Straight") is formed, as its name denotes, by skipping pips in sequence. A sample hand—Two, Four, Six, Eight, Ten. The Ace here is counted as one only. In the order of merit, this combination takes precedence over a Two Pair, and also over a Blaze.

ROUND THE CORNER is a freak form of Straight or Sequence, in which the Ace plays the dual rôle of One and Thirteen—"Alpha" and "Omega," as one might say. It forms an intermediate card between the King and the Deuce, simultaneously acting as the highest and lowest, as in Queen, King, Ace, Two and Three. The combination ranks after Threes and below the regular Straight.

THE JOKER

Having mentioned the Joker, we will now proceed to explain the part it plays or may play in the game. Many players object to the introduction of this fifty-third card, in the belief that it stultifies the betting; invariably, therefore, before play starts, the company vote as to whether it should be included. When it is brought into play, the Joker is the most coveted card in the pack, for the holder can call it any card that suits him. Even, if his other four cards are rubbish, he remains in the draw, as whatever happens, he is always assured of a Pair at least. With the Joker in action, the possibilities of improving a hand are increased two-fold, and as a consequence its presence has a steadying influence on speculation, even with the holder of a natural Full Hand. High counting hands become prolific—supposing you draw four cards to the Joker, and pick up Two Pair, say a Pair of Jacks and a Pair of Fives. That is transformed into a Full Hand—Three Jacks and a Pair of Fives. Two Aces along with the Joker and any Pair is an unbeatable Full Hand, because it is impossible for an opponent also to hold three Aces. This all-powerful fifty-third card goes to form many Straights, Flushes and Straight Flushes; and if you are born with Four Aces, and for your discard, you secure the Joker, you, on a show of hands, declare Fives! Five Aces is, of course, top-weight in any form of the game; but, though it is extremely rare, it is generally agreed upon at the start of play that if any Five does occur and happens by some miracle to be up against a natural Royal Flush, the latter takes precedence. An Ace, King, Queen, Jack, Ten Royal Flush should always be classed as the only invulnerable hand.

JACK POTS

With the idea of making the game more varied, the Jack Pot is generally introduced into ordinary Poker. Briefly, a Jack Pot is a special pool to which all players contribute an equal amount before the cards are dealt, and when Jack Pots are being played no betting can take place until a player claims the necessary qualification, viz., the possession of a pair of Jacks or better.

Jack Pots may, by agreement, be declared at any time, or to follow any particular winning combination; but a usual method is to decide that each time the deal comes round to the player winning the opening hand, a Jack Pot shall be played. He is handed a "Buck" (any convenient article, say a pocket-knife) which, when his turn has come to deal, he places in the centre of the table as a reminder to the company in general. Simultaneously all the players place an agreed amount in the Pot. Keeping to our £1 as a betting limit, the first contribution to the Pot should be 3s. All having paid, the deal is proceeded with, and then the player on the left (Ante-man is temporarily abolished) declares whether he will open the Pot, or pass. As already mentioned, the opener must have a pair of Jacks or a better combination in his hand. No one is compelled to open even if he is qualified, and if he does not, or cannot, open it, he retains his cards, for he is allowed to come in, if he wishes, after the Pot has been opened by someone else.

Supposing all pass, each player puts a "refresher" or "fattener" in the Pot (on our betting maximum basis, say 1s.) and the same dealer deals again, the same process of opening being repeated. If this time still no one opens, another "refresher" of a shilling is placed in the centre—making 5s. each, which is our agreed limit. Should there be further abortive attempts at opening, no further "refreshers" are put up. When the Pot is opened the opener places in the Pool any amount he chooses within the agreed limit (say 3s., 4s. or 5s.) for single bets. Then after the usual draw, betting proceeds as in ordinary Poker—excepting that the opener starts the wagering, and the next player in turn must either see, raise, or throw in.

If before the betting has concluded the opener decides not to see any raise, he must expose his hand before throwing in, in order to prove that he had the qualifying openers; other players, as they drop out, throw their cards face down. There is the possibility of a player accidentally opening without having the desired qualification, and should he discover his error before the discarding, it is the general practice to declare his hand foul, in which case he forfeits whatever amount he has placed in the Pot, and those who have already paid their deposits continue with the game. Should it transpire, on a show of hands to ascertain who is the winner of the Pot, that the opener has inferior to a Pair of Jacks, he is penalized to the extent of double the whole of the pool, a severe but necessary penalty.

The winner of the Jack Pot having been declared, he takes the pool, along with the Buck, which he retains, until his turn arrives to deal—another Jack Pot.

It occasionally arises that a Jack Pot opener desires to "split" his openers. For instance he may have the Jack of Clubs, the Jack of Hearts and three other Hearts. Here is a possible Flush, so he draws only one card, discarding the Jack of Clubs, placing it by his side for future reference, at the same time announcing that he has split his openers. This is a wise manœuvre when the opposition is numerically strong.

Another little piece of advice: when a Jack Pot opener has an exceptionally good hand, he should make his preliminary bet as light as possible, so as to entice the others in, even to the extent of raising him. If, however, he has only the bare openers, it is generally considered advisable to open for the limit, on the principle "the smaller the opposition the better the chance of winning." Finally, it is a golden rule to open the Jack Pot whenever you can, even if you are the first man called upon.

OTHER VARIATIONS

WHISKY POKER introduces an extra hand, called "the Widow." The player on the left of the dealer has the first option of taking this pack, failing him, the next on the left and so on. Whoever takes "the Widow" must place his original cards face upwards, when the next player on the left can take any or all of these exposed cards, replacing them by as many as he takes. If no one takes the Widow, the draw, one card at a time, takes place. As soon as a player decides that he has a hand good enough to stand on, he signifies the fact by rapping on the table. Then the other players have one other single card draw, if they desire. Finally, the hands are considered "called" and the highest wins.

TABLE STAKES savours a little of Straddling. Each player puts up any stake he pleases, and when it happens that they are of uneven value, a player may "call a sight" upon a lower bet. Say, for example A has put down 5s., but B has only 3s. in front of him. He "calls a sight," by putting his 3s. in the Pool. Then A removes from the pool the difference between the two bets, and places that sum apart from other money. Now C may appear on the scene by producing 3s. to balance B, and he can even raise if he likes. Suppose he raises A 2s., he must put 4s. more into the Pool, making his stake 7s. If A does not see his way to cover this bet he retires, and further interest in the proceedings is confined to B and C. If B's hand is better than C's, he rakes in the Pool up to the value of his own bet, but C would take everything above that level, such, for instance, as A's two extra shillings.

STUD POKER resolves itself into speculating while the deal is in progress. The first card to each player is handed face down, and the second exposed. The player with the highest exposed card glances at his unknown card, and decides whether he will bet or not. If he will not, he retires; if, on the other hand, he bets, the player next him must see him, or throw in. Then, to those who remain in play, a third exposed card is handed, then a fourth, and then a fifth—when the Hand with the best combination takes the Pool.

FLAT POKER is the simplest of all variations. There is no fixed ante-money ("Blind"), but the Age planks down whatever stake he pleases within a prescribed limit. Other players must cover what he deposits—or drop out. There is no Straddle, Ante, or Raise, and after the deal and discarding, any player can back his hand against the Table, meaning that he must increase his bet to the total amount paid in by all the other players taken together. There are no raises—only the player who is backing his hand can be seen, and the best hand wins.

Those who realise the many subtle points with which ordinary Poker bristles, may be pardoned for remarking that this particular variety of play is aptly named—FLAT!

VINGT-ET-UN

VINGT-ET-UN is a round game in which any number may take part, though six or seven participants probably make the best "school." A complete pack of cards is used; there are no trumps, and the cards have no relative rank, as the object of the game is to hold cards the complete pip value of which is twenty-one (Fr., *vingt-et-un*), or as near as possible to that value without exceeding it. Aces count either 1 or 11 at the choice of the holder, Kings, Queens, Jacks and Tens 10 each, and the remaining cards the number of their respective pips.

Each player should start with the same number of counters, and the limit of the stake having been decided on, cards are dealt for dealer, the deal going to the player receiving the first Ace. In some schools betting now takes place, each player except the dealer putting up either an agreed amount or any stake not exceeding the limit; in others one card is dealt all round and seen by the player to whom it is dealt before a bet is made; but in all each player is dealt two cards, one at a time.

The dealer himself makes no bet, but acts as Banker, taking or paying—as the case may be—all bets made by the others. When betting does not take place until the first card is seen, he is, however, allowed, after seeing his own card, to call on the players to double their stakes, and it is only the dealer who has this privilege.

Each player now examines his cards, and if the dealer has a "natural," viz., an Ace with a court card or Ten, each pays him double the amount of his stake (or the doubled stake). If a player also holds a natural the usual procedure is that the holder pays dealer the original (or doubled) stake and the deal passes to him, except in the case of the first hand of a deal. If a player should hold a natural and the dealer none, then the dealer pays the player double—or, in some schools, three times the stake. If no one has received a natural, and also after any player other than dealer has been paid for a natural held, each in turn, beginning with player on dealer's left, may ask for a third (or as many cards as he may desire, one after the other) with the object of bringing his pip value as near 21 as possible. In some schools these additional cards are paid for with any sum not exceeding the stake.

Suppose, for instance, the player's original holding amounts to 12 only, he asks for another card and receives a deuce, making 14, so he has another, this time an Ace which, as we have seen, counts either as 1 or 11. He, of course, gives it the value of 1, making his total 15 only, so he has another; if this happens to be a six he declares a natural and is paid; if its value is over 6 he " bursts," i.e., throws his cards in and pays up; if it is a four or a five (making 19 or 20) he would be well advised to stand. Drawing proceeds in this way until each player is " content " or has " burst "; the dealer then turns his cards face up and draws. If he overdraws he pays each player still in the amount of his stake; if he draws 21 or less he takes from those holding less and pays those holding more, while in ties neither side pays (though in some schools ties are paid to the dealer, and in some, again, the dealer receives double stakes for 21).

SPLITTING

SPLITTING. Any player, other than the dealer, holding two Aces (or, in some circles, any pair) may " split " them, make a bet on each, and draw to each in turn.

A natural drawn on a split hand counts double, unless the dealer also draws a natural, in which case no money passes.

THE DEAL. Change of deal is effected by various methods. In one, after the first hand, the deal passes to the player first making a natural. In another a definite number of deals, or the winning or losing of a definite amount by the dealer, is decided upon beforehand; in yet another the dealer retains the bank until the pack is exhausted—either once or twice, as may be arranged; while it may pass to the left in turn after each round.

After one deal the next is made with the remainder of the pack, and when the whole pack has been dealt out the discards are gathered and shuffled, and the deal continued.

VINGT-ET-UN VARIATIONS

VINGT-ET-UN is such a simple and popular game that there can be little wonder that it has given rise to a number of variations, some of which are played only in one locality and quite a number of which have, in their turn, been the origin of further local divergencies. Here we have space to mention only a few of them—and first we would say that PONTOON, so well known to our soldiers on all fronts during the World War, was the common name for Vingt-et-Un or some one of its varieties which happened to be popular in any given locality or at any given period. Pontoon was never, at all times and in all places, a game limited by definite rules as is, say, Whist or Cribbage. The only rules were that "21" had to be made in one or other of the recognized ways, and that if you were caught attempting to make the magic score in any way not recognized by the particular school, well, you had to have some ready explanation—or you were "for it"!

Another general name attached to the game, viz., FRENCH VINGT-ET-UN, may be dismissed in a few words. Why this particular version should be so decisively given a nationality when the original game is already clearly labelled French, no one has ever been able to discover, but the name is applied to a game that is played with each variation in successive hands. The first hand is invariably played according to the rules of the "straight" game as detailed on pp. 135-7; for the succeeding hands the following variations are employed, one after the other, in any order that may previously have been agreed.

ANTIPATHY AND SYMPATHY. When the stakes have been made each player is asked in turn by the dealer whether he chooses "Antipathy" or "Sympathy," and when the choice has been made two cards are dealt to each. Those who have called "Antipathy" win if the cards they have been dealt are of different colours, while the "Sympathy" callers lose unless their cards are of the same colour. Losers pay to, and winners receive from, the dealer according to their stakes.

CLOCK. In this variation the dealer deals the cards (after the usual shuffling and cutting) face upwards in a circle in front of him, calling the cards in numerical order as he does so—One to the first, Two to the second, Three to the third, and so on, until he reaches Thirteen for the King, when he starts again at One. If during the call-over the pip-value of any card tallies with the number called, e.g., if the third card exposed is a three or the twelfth a Queen—the dealer wins the agreed stake from each player. If, on the other hand, the dealer reaches Thirteen without any card having tallied he pays a like amount to each player.

Dealer should go through the whole pack, no matter how many times he has lost or won.

ODD OR EVEN. Here the player, after having made his stake, makes choice of "Odd" or "Even," whereupon he is dealt one card. If the pip-value (J, Q and K being numbered 11, 12 and 13) corresponds with his choice he wins and is paid; if not he loses. A variation of this variation is ROUGE ET NOIR in which "Black" and "Red" are the options, and in either it is the rule in some schools to deal three cards instead of one, when the number or colour, as the case may be, of two out of three of them decides the winner.

COMPANY AND SELF. After the stakes have been made the dealer deals two cards, one for himself and one for "the Rest" or "the Company." If they happen to form a pair he wins, if not he goes on dealing the cards (one by one and face up) until one is turned which pairs with one or the other of the two lay-out cards. If it is with his own card that the turned card pairs, he wins, if it is with the other he loses and pays out all round.

DIFFERENCES. Here the dealer deals two cards, in rotation, face upwards to each player, and two to himself. Dealer pays out on all hands that are higher than his own and receives from all that are lower, at a previously agreed rate. Aces count as 1 only, and in the event of a tie no money passes. This form of the game is also known as PAY AND RECEIVE.

PA, MA, AND THE BABY. In this variation we have an additional complication, and a chance of making—or losing—larger money. The Ace ("Baby") is valued only at 1; naturals (which, as throughout, total 21) consisting of any combination other than K, Q, Ace pay and receive double, and "Pa, Ma, and the Baby" (K, Q, Ace) four times the stake-value. The play and procedure are otherwise as in ordinary Vingt-et-Un.

BACCARAT

BACCARAT is another banking game, like Vingt-et-Un, in which one player is continually opposed to all the others; indeed, it is a kind of glorified Vingt-et-Un, the chief differences being in the pip-value aimed at, and in the fact that whatever is the number of the banker's opponents he has only two hands opposing him.

There are two varieties—the ordinary Baccarat, or *Baccarat à deux tableaux*, and *Baccarat Chemin de Fer.* As the differences between the two are by no means fundamental we will first describe the ordinary game, and then give the other as a variation.

Any number from three to eleven may take part, and the bank goes to the highest bidder, that is, to the one who will put up the largest sum of money to be played for. The others cut for seats at the table, the lowest taking the seat on the banker's right, the next lowest that on his left, and the others in the same way, right and left alternately. The table is divided longitudinally down the centre (hence the " à deux tableaux "), and when the banker has a croupier to assist him in watching the bets, gathering and shuffling the cards, etc., he sits opposite him at the other end of this line. In the middle of the table is a waste-basket into which used cards are thrown.

The object of the game is to hold cards the total value of which most closely approaches 8 or 9, an 8 made with two cards taking precedence of a 9 made with three. Court cards and 10s count nothing; all the others, including the Aces, are reckoned at their pip-value. Three complete packs of cards are shuffled together (the banker having the right of last shuffle) and used as one.

Players having taken their seats, the amount bid for the bank is placed on the table and bets are made on the right and left of the table before the deal begins, in any amount the players please, so long as the total sum does not exceed the capital in the bank at the time. It is no good going beyond this—for such bets will not be paid; and if a player betting on the side of the table opposite to that at which he is sitting wins, he is not paid until settlement has been made with all the players at that side. Further, any player may bet on both sides at once—*à cheval*, as it is called—by placing his stake on the centre-line; in this case the punter wins if both sides win, and loses if both sides lose, while if one side wins and the other loses no money passes.

The cards having been shuffled and cut the banker spreads them face downward in front of him and slips off the top card, handing it to the player on his right, face down. Then he gives the next card to the player on his left, and then the next to himself; he does this once more, and then the three players examine their two cards. If any of the three finds he holds 8 or 9 he must show it at once, and the two other hands are then exposed; if it is the banker who holds them and neither of his opponents has as many, the bank takes all the stakes; if either punter has more than the banker the bank pays all the bets on that side of the table; if either has less, all bets on that side are lost; and if either ties with the banker, the bets on that side are a stand-off, neither winning nor losing.

If on this first deal no one can claim 8 or 9 the banker offers the top card of the pack, face down, to the player on his right. If it is refused it is offered to the player on his left, and if again it is refused the banker must take it himself. If it is accepted by the player on the right, player on the left has the option of asking for a card also, but whether or not he exercises this option, once the first card offered has been accepted the banker is not obliged to take one himself, though he may if he likes. Only one draw is allowed; any card drawn is at once turned face up in front of its drawer, and when the drawing is completed all the hands are exposed. The banker now pays all bets on the side of a punter holding cards nearer to 9 than his own, and takes on the side holding cards not so near as his, ties being, as before, a stand-off.

This finishes the "coup," and when all bets are paid the used cards are thrown into the waste-basket and stakes placed for the next coup. There is no more shuffling or cutting; the banker deals from the top of the stock to the player on his right if he has just won, but to the next player beyond him if he has lost, and then to the left side of the table in the same way. This goes on at each deal until all the players have held cards and have lost a coup, when the deal starts again at the player nearest the banker. There must be at least ten cards in the stock when the last deal is made.

If the banker loses all he has, the bank is put up for auction and goes to the highest bidder, and if the banker at any time retires the next banker must put into the bank an amount equal to that then in it.

There is one other point that should be mentioned, and that is the call of Banco. This is an offer to the banker to play for his whole capital at a single coup; it takes precedence of all other propositions, and may be made by either player before the cards are dealt. If the bank wins, the same or any player may repeat the challenge on the next coup—now, of course, worth double the previous amount—but no player may offer Banco more than twice in succession. If the bank loses it is put up for auction and passes to the highest bidder.

CHEMIN DE FER

In this variation of Baccarat it is usual to play with six packs of cards, shuffled together, and the bank passes to the next player on the left as soon as the banker loses a coup. The banker gives cards only to the player on his right and to himself, so he must either win or lose at each deal. If the player to whom the card is given does not go Banco, any player beyond him may do so, in order; if Banco is not called, players, going in turn to the right, make any bets they please not together exceeding the capital in the bank.

If the banker wins he deals again; if he loses the bank and deal pass to the player on his left. He may, however, after winning a coup, pass the deal to the player on his right if that player will put into the bank as much as it then contains; if that is done, when the coup is next lost the bank passes to the player to whom it would have gone had it not been transferred.

It will be seen from this brief account of the game that Baccarat calls for nothing in the way of intellectual effort, but is simply a means of passing the time and of risking, maybe, considerable sums of money. It also, and it is only fair to mention this, gives almost endless opportunities to the clever rogue, and it is said that few who know anything of sharp practice at cards can resist the temptation of cheating at Baccarat. Once this is realized one has only oneself to blame if, through joining a Baccarat school composed even partly of strangers, one loses more than is convenient.

Cheating at Baccarat is by no means confined to the class of race-goer who induces strangers to "spot the lady" on the way to the course. There was a very celebrated law-case towards the end of the last century that arose from misplaying this game. The form of dishonesty practised, more than once, by the gentleman who was caught red-handed when Royalty was present, consisted simply in laying the stake so close to the line as to be nearly *à cheval* and then, when it was fairly obvious which side had lost, giving it the little push that would send it on the line and so save it if the other side won! So simple; so thoroughly exposed; and yet, even to-day, so often tried!

NAPOLEON

NAPOLEON (known more familiarly to English-speaking players as "Nap") is a round game, played with no partners, and by any number from two to six, or even seven. Five members probably make the best "school," and it should be borne in mind that the smaller the number the better the chances of successful calls, as the combinations and the cards against any individual hand are fewer. The cards have the same value as at Whist; Ace highest, deuce lowest. Dealing takes place from the complete pack, this having been first shuffled (dealer having right of final shuffle) and cut, but five cards only are dealt to each player, and they may be dealt either singly, two-three, or three-two, as previously decided.

The object of the game is to win tricks by the run of the cards. The right to first deal having been decided in the usual way and the cards having been dealt, all players examine their hands and the player on the dealer's left makes the first call, *i.e.* declares how many tricks he will attempt to score—two, three, four, or five—the latter call being known as "Nap." A call of one is not allowed; neither is a call of two, in most schools of four or over. If first player's hand is not sufficiently strong to warrant a call he "passes," and it is his left-hand neighbour's turn to make a declaration. So the calling goes round to each player, and whoever makes the highest bid plays his hand against the rest. Players have the opportunity of making one bid only, and if all pass, the hands are thrown in and there is a fresh deal (by the next dealer), the stakes for this hand usually being doubled.

THE PLAY. The winner of the declaration has the first lead, and the suit of the card he leads is the trump suit for that hand; his opponents play to it in turn and *must follow suit* if possible; otherwise a discard must be played to the first trick, and to any subsequent trick either trump or discard. The highest card of suit led, or highest trump played against it, wins, and the winner of one trick leads to the next. When the hands are played out and the points scored, the cards are gathered, shuffled with the complete pack, and re-dealt by next dealer for the next hand. Tricks as taken are turned face down and arranged so that they can be easily counted; once turned and quitted they cannot be re-examined.

The declarer who makes his declaration takes from each of the other players whatever stake is being played, multiplied by the number of tricks called (and no more, although he may have scored more); while if he loses he pays each opponent the same amount—unless the call has been "Nap" (5 tricks) in which case he receives double the stakes from each on winning, but pays out only single stakes if he loses. Thus a call of three at the popular "penny Nap" results either in the caller taking 3d. from, or paying 3d. to, each opponent, while if the call is "Nap" and he wins, he takes 10d. (more usually 1s. 0d.) from each on winning, and pays out 5d. (or 6d.) only to each if he is so unfortunate as to lose.

To become an expert at "Nap" one must learn, first, how to estimate the value of one's hand—taking into consideration the number of the school and the character of previous calls (if any); and, second, how to play the hand—either as declarer or opponent—so as to get the best results from it. Both are matters of experience, and the person with "card sense" and a slight acquaintance with Whist will have small difficulty in acquiring it. For instance, first caller holding Ace of Hearts; King, 5 of Spades; Queen of Diamonds; and 10 of Clubs, would be well advised to pass (his hand is a better "stopper" than winner); but holding same hand as fourth or fifth caller, the others having passed, he might risk a call of three. In this case he would play his King of Spades and, if this "got home," follow with Queen of Diamonds, counting on making his Ace of Hearts, and trumping Diamonds or Hearts when next led. Playing as opponent it is, of course, wasteful to take a small lead with an Ace or a trump if other players are to follow, but even this depends upon the state of the game, and whether or not the caller is on the point of making his declaration. Always remember, too, that the number of the players has a great effect on the way in which one can call and should play. With five in the school the odds against any player holding a card not in your own hand is just about 9 to 7; with 3 in the school they are considerably greater, and with 6 or 7, less. Bearing this in mind, it becomes comparatively easy, after the first round, to estimate the probable number of trumps against one; trump strength is, of course, of the greatest value, and the Ace, if held, should invariably be the first lead. "Three" is a very popular call; but care is needed here in discarding, for a suit of two may be very useful after trumps have been drawn.

IRREGULARITIES AND PENALTIES: Revoking. A detected revoke at once stops the play of the hand; a revoking caller pays each opponent the amount of his bid; a revoking opponent pays that amount to the caller for himself and for each of the opponents.

MISDEAL. Player holding incorrect number of cards must claim a misdeal before bidding or passing; if he fails to do so hands must be played as dealt. If bidder holds correct number of cards and is successful he is paid, but if he fails, no money passes. If bidder holds incorrect number, he scores nothing for winning when holding more than he should, but pays or receives if holding less, losing any trick to which he has no card to play.

LEADING OUT OF TURN. Bidder is not penalised, but must take back card led unless all have played to it, in which case the lead stands. Opponent leading out of turn pays bidder three counters, and forfeits his winnings if bidder loses.

"NAP" VARIATIONS

There are many variations to "Nap," and while all of them have been introduced with the idea of making the game "better and brighter" many of them are adopted only by particular clubs or schools. Here we can notice only a few, the first among which are "Wellington" and

"Blucher," which are merely the names for doubling and trebling the stakes for a call of "Nap." The first can only be made when "Nap" has already been called, and the second when "Wellington" has been called, and the larger call, of course, displaces the smaller. "Misery" or "Misère" (adopted from "Solo"), is another variation; the call ranks above "Three" but below "Four," and is paid for as a "Three." There are no trumps, and if the caller takes a single trick he has lost.

In "Peep Nap," a "Nap" caller is allowed to look at the top card and exchange it for one held should he desire to do so, and the "Floater" is an extension of this idea. When the hands have been dealt an extra card is laid face down on the table, and the players may look at it in turn, paying a small stake for the privilege, the pool so formed going to the next winner of a "Nap" call. There is no obligation to take the floater, but when taken the discard becomes the floater for any succeeding player who may like to pay for the "peep." In another variation any player who cares to pay for the privilege may look at the floater before calling commences, and then each calls as though it were one of his cards. The highest caller takes it, discarding a card from his hand, and play proceeds in the ordinary manner.

In some schools it is the practice to start off with a "Kitty," or pool, into which each player puts a small stake, to which additions are made each round, and also by any player failing in his bid. The stake is usually one counter for each trick called, and when the player "goes down" he pays out all round and puts the same amount in the pool.

Again some schools heighten the interest by dealing an extra hand of five cards. The players, after examining their hands, have in rotation the option of adding them to their own and of selecting from the ten cards a hand of five which they play. In this form of the game "Nap" is the only call, except that if the players all pass, the dealer has the option of taking the extra hand—paying a stake in the pool for this privilege—when he is obliged to make a call of some sort.

LOO

THERE are several varieties of this once most popular of all round games of cards, but the best known form is "Three Card Loo," "Limited" or "Unlimited," and this will be first described. There is no difference in the play of the "Limited" and "Unlimited" varieties of the game, the limitation affecting only the stakes, in a manner which is described below.

THREE CARD LOO. The complete pack of fifty-two cards is used, these ranking as at Whist—Ace highest, deuce lowest—and as the game is played with a pool into which an agreed number of counters, either three, or some multiple of three, is paid, each player should be provided with chips of two colours, white, say, representing one point, and red three. One player should act as banker throughout, selling and redeeming the chips, and supervising the pool; any number from three to seventeen may play, but five or six make the best game and the usual limit is eight.

The dealer, who is selected by cutting or otherwise (first knave in a faced deal is a good method), first places the agreed stake in the pool and then deals three cards to each player, one at a time, beginning with player on his left, and an extra hand (the "Widow" or "Miss") immediately before his own; the top card on remainder of the pack after all hands have been dealt is turned up and decides the trump suit. In the event of a misdeal, or of a card being exposed during a deal, dealer pays three counters (or whatever has been agreed upon as the stake) into the pool. This penalty also applies to revokes and other irregularities.

The deal being finished, the dealer asks each player in rotation, beginning on his left, to declare, and no player may look at his cards until so asked. The player has three alternatives; he may either "stand," i.e., play with the cards dealt him; or "take the widow," i.e., exchange his cards for the extra hand ; or " pass," i.e., retire from the game for that round. In either of the last two cases the original hand is not shown, but either placed face down in the middle of the table or given to the dealer who puts it at the bottom of the pack ; while if the player stands or takes the widow, he is bound to take at least one trick or be " looed," i.e., pay an amount equal to the original stake into the pool to form the pool for the next hand. If the widow is declined, the offer is made to the next player, and so on in rotation ; once it is taken the remaining players must either stand or pass.

If one player takes the widow and the others pass, he takes the pool without having to play for it ; and should only one player stand, the widow not having been taken, the dealer must either play his own cards, or take the widow and play it either on his own account or to defend the pool ; i.e., any winnings he may make go to the pool for the next round and not to himself, while if he fails to take a trick he is not looed. If all but the dealer pass, the dealer takes the pool.

The player nearest the dealer's left among those who have not passed now leads a card ; he must lead a trump if he has one (the rule used to be " if he holds two or more ") ; if he holds the Ace of trumps (either with others or " bare ") he must lead it ; also, if the trump-card is an Ace and he holds the King of that suit he must lead it. Further, if he is pitted against only one other player and holds more than one trump he must lead the highest, unless his highest are in sequence (counting or not counting in the turn-up card), in which case he may lead either. The other players follow in rotation, and must not only follow suit but " head the trick," i.e., play a higher card of the suit, if able to do so. If unable to follow suit he must trump, and if the trick is already trumped, over-trump, if he can do so, but he need not under-trump. The winner of the trick leads to the next, and is bound by the same rules as to leading a trump, etc., as the original leader.

Hands having been played out, the winner of each trick takes one-third of the pool for each trick he has won, and any player who has failed to take a trick is 'looed' (see above); but if only three players are left in on any hand, and each takes one trick, no "loo-ing" is possible, and the next round's pool consists only of the new dealer's stake. In such an event the common practice is to play this next hand as a "must," in which there is no widow and everybody is obliged to play whatever cards he holds, with the result that a pool consisting of contributions from all but three of the players is built up again.

A variation to Three-card Loo is adopted in many circles by giving a special value to a flush. As soon as the dealer has declared, the holder of three trumps asks him "How many playing?" and, on the reply being given, shows his flush and claims the pool, each player "in" being looed. If two players hold flushes in trumps the elder hand wins, irrespective of pip-value, but the younger hand is not looed.

FIVE-CARD LOO. In Five-card Loo there is no widow; each player is dealt five cards, either singly or in the Écarté method (three-two or two-three); and the contribution to the pool must be *five* chips or a multiple thereof; the top card on remainder of pack after dealing gives the trump suit, as in the Three-card game.

The deal being completed, the dealer asks each player in turn, beginning on his left, whether or not he will play and, if he will, how many cards, if any, he would like to exchange; each may exchange as many as he pleases—but cannot alter in any way the number first asked for—and discarded cards may not be seen by other players; once having decided to play one cannot withdraw.

The rules as to leading, following suit, heading the trick, flushes (five cards in this case, of course), etc., are the same as in the Three-card game, but there is an additional variation for the Knave of Clubs which is—in the words of Alexander Pope—promoted into:

Mighty PAM, that Kings and Queens o'erthrew,
And mow'd down armies in the fights of Loo.

Pam is a super-trump, a Trump of Trumps; it takes precedence even over the Ace of the trump suit, and is four of a suit and Pam are held in one hand, it acts as a Joker, turning the four into a flush. There is only one limitation to his power, and that is that if the Ace of trumps is led Pam must not be played if its holder can retain it without revoking.

The chief remaining varieties in this fine old game are "Irish" or "Draw Loo," and the playing of "Club Law." The latter can be applied to any variety of this game, and has the effect of obliging everybody to play, and to play on his own cards without drawing or taking the widow, when Clubs are trumps.

IRISH LOO is played with three cards, without a widow, and the laws of the ordinary game are observed; but any player electing to come in is allowed to exchange all or any of his cards for others. He may only do this once, as in the Five-card game; indeed, Irish Loo is practically Five-card Loo played with only three cards, and, as will be apparent, either variety gives much greater scope for high play and gambling than the "straight" game. For this reason both should always be played "Limited."

LIMITED AND UNLIMITED. As remarked at the opening of this article, "limitation" at Loo does not affect the deal or play in any way, but merely the amounts paid into the pool. In *Limited Loo* the penalty is always the agreed number of chips—three or five, or a multiple thereof; in *Unlimited Loo* the same penalty is paid for irregularities, revokes and so forth, but a player on being 'looed' has to pay into the pool an amount equal to that in it at the time. By this method of play very large sums accumulate—and can be lost or won—with great rapidity as two or more fail on successive deals, and it is only when there are but three players in, and each takes a trick, that the pool can be brought back to its normal size. Indulgence in Unlimited Loo is not recommended to anybody; and even those to whom the loss of a few thousands is a matter of no consequence are usually careful in their choice of company when playing "Unlimited," and fix a maximum which cannot be exceeded.

SLIPPERY SAM

THIS is another of those Round Games in which almost any number of players can take part and, partly because of this, and partly because of its simplicity, it is very popular in the family circle. It is a development of "Blind Hookey" in which the players each cut in turn from a single pack of cards and bet "blind" (i.e., without previous inspection) on the value of the bottom card, and it is played with the ordinary pack of fifty-two cards, these ranking as at Whist—Ace highest, deuce lowest.

The dealer (who is also the banker) having been selected, either by cutting or by some other method, places in the pool as many counters as he wishes to form the bank. The cards are now shuffled and cut in the usual way, and the banker deals each punter—i.e., all the players except himself—three cards face downwards. The punters examine their hands and play commences by the player on dealer's left staking all or some proportion of the counters in the pool on the chance of there being one card among his three of higher value in the same suit than the present top card of the pack (not the bottom card, as in "Blind Hookey") though he may, of course, refuse to back his chances, in which case the call passes to his left-hand neighbour. When a punter has made his stake, the banker turns the top card. If the punter wins he is paid out, if he loses, his stake goes into the pool. As noted above, it is only in the suit of the top card that the banker can be beaten; if this happens to be the deuce of Clubs, and the punter holds, say, the Aces or Kings in Hearts, Diamonds, and Spades, the punter has to pay.

So the banker goes to each player in turn, and as the paying to or receiving from each, as the case may be, is concluded, punters' cards and the then top card are thrown into the rubbish-heap, the next card in the stock being the top card for the next punter. As the pack gets low the rubbish-heap is collected by player to dealer's right and, after being shuffled and cut, is handed to him and placed below any remaining cards he may have in hand.

There is no definite rule about the passing of the bank; this is generally decided before play commences by the players themselves, but it is usual for one to retain the bank for three complete rounds, with the option of continuing for one round further, but no more; and always with the proviso that if the pool should be drained dry the bank at once passes to player on banker's left, unless it has previously been arranged that the banker may, at his discretion, add up to some definite amount to the emptied bank.

It is advisable to limit the amount of a punter's stake to the amount originally put into the pool by the banker, and for the following reason; suppose the banker starts with twelve chips and has a run of luck, by the time the fourth or fifth punter has gone down he will have quite a respectable amount in the pool—60 or 70 chips, perhaps. Next punter, feeling either reckless or wealthy, if left a free hand, may easily scoop the lot, and in practice it will be found that to restrain him as above makes, as a rule, for better harmony.

Note that it is never worth while to bet heavily on a one-suited hand, for it will go down before any card of one of the other suits. With two suits one need not be so careful, while when holding nines or over of three different suits, one can afford to plunge a bit. The best hand is one of three Aces; but even that, as we have seen, may be beaten by a deuce of the suit not held.

NEWMARKET

NEWMARKET, also known as "Stops," and "Boodle," is a modern version of the old game of "Pope Joan," and in its simplified form is a great favourite in family circles. Any number from three to eight can participate, and it is played with one complete pack of cards (ranking from Ace up to King) with an additional King of Hearts, Jack of Diamonds, Queen of Clubs and Ace of Spades (or some other high card in place of the latter) from another pack to form the "lay-out" or, according to American terminology, the "Boodle cards." These are laid face upwards, and before the deal the dealer places his stake (at least four counters) on them or on any of them in any way he pleases; each other player must put up an equivalent stake, but he can divide it among the Boodle cards exactly as his taste and fancy directs. The objects of the game are, firstly, to be the first to get rid of one's cards and, secondly, to play cards corresponding to the Boodle cards.

THE BOODLE CARDS

The cards are dealt one at a time to the left in the usual way, but the dealer starts by dealing to an extra hand, then to himself, and then to the others in rotation. The cards of the extra hand are known as the "bafflers," for their use is to provide "stops," and they are never exposed.

THE PLAY. Player on dealer's left commences; he may lead from any suit, but it must be the lowest card in that suit, and he must then play any card or cards he holds in that suit that are in ascending sequence. When he has finished, the player, if any, able to continue the sequence does so, and this goes on until a " stop " occurs, either through the King or a card that is in the " dead hand " having been reached. When this happens the player of the last card continues by playing the lowest card of another suit, unless he holds only the suit just stopped, in which case he plays the lowest in that. He who plays any card corresponding to a Boodle card takes the stakes on it, and the game is ended when a player has got rid of all his cards. His reward is as many counters from each player as each holds cards, and any stakes remaining on the Boodle cards at the finish go to increase the stakes on the next round.

In the play a leader holding a card corresponding to a Boodle card will, of course, lead off with the lowest of that suit; and it is to a player's advantage to get rid of low cards in a previously stopped suit just as soon as he can.

PENALTIES. There are one or two penalties in Newmarket that should be noted. If a player who has made a " stop " leads from the same suit when holding cards in another, or if he leads any card other than his lowest in the suit he leads, he forfeits one counter to each player. The same penalty is exacted from a player who fails to continue a sequence when he can do so; while if the card he has held up is the next lower to a Boodle card he pays the holder of the corresponding card the amount staked on it, or, if the corresponding card is in the " dead hand," puts it on the Boodle card.

RUMMY

RUMMY is always a very popular game, especially in the family circle. It is played with the full pack of cards (sometimes including the Joker), and by any number of players from two to six, four being probably the best. The object of each player is to get rid as quickly as possible of all the cards dealt him, by laying them out in threes or fours (combinations), or in sequence and suit of three or more (sequences).

Variations are many, for almost every district has a different code of rules, but all systems are based on the directions here given, and the reader who familiarizes himself with them will be able to join any circle without having to learn much that is new.

In two-hand Rummy 10 cards are dealt to each ; in three-hand 7, and in four or more 6. They are dealt one at a time ; the next card is laid face up in the centre of the table, and the remainder of the pack (the " stock ") face down beside it.

The deal being completed, each player sorts his cards into as many combinations and sequences as he holds, and then in turn, beginning with player on dealer's left, must take either the card from the top of the stock, without showing it, or the faced card beside the stock, or one of the cards that have become exposed (as under) in course of play. For this card he discards one already held, and this becomes a faced card and can be taken in exchange by another player. In one variety of Rummy the game is made longer by the rule that all discards must be laid on top of the original exposed card. Having exchanged, the player may lay any one sequence or combination he holds on the table in front of him, and the succeeding players follow in the same way, and may also get rid of one card by adding it to a sequence already laid down.

Rounds continue in this way, the stock being turned

and played through again if necessary, until one player wins by getting rid of all the cards dealt to or drawn by him. This he does, either by laying them all on the table, or by laying out some, giving others to other players' lay-outs and discarding the last. He is then paid by the other players according to the number of pips on the cards left in their hands, Ace counting 1, and the court cards 11, 12 and 13. It will be seen from this method of scoring that it is wise to get rid of one's high value sequences and combinations at the earliest opportunity.

When the Joker is used its acquisition may alter the whole prospect of one's hand. If, for instance, one holds 10, J of a suit, two 7s, and various, and the Joker is picked up, it can be used either as another 7, making the combination; or as 9 or Q, making a sequence.

SEQUENCE—10, J, Q COMBINATION—THREE 7S

Neither need, of course, be laid out at once, and it often pays to hold on for a draw or two on the chance of increasing the sequence or picking up another 7 and so releasing the Joker for other purposes.

In many schools the Joker is rather frowned upon as not being in the pure "card spirit." In others, however, the additional excitement it provides has proved to be so delightful that all the deuces are turned into Jokers, making five in all, and there is no denying that this gives a lively game!

RUMMY VARIATIONS

The following are, perhaps, the best of the many variations to which we have referred above; they may be played by three or more (seven being a reasonable limit), and when five or more are taking part two packs, well shuffled together, are used.

Eight cards are dealt to each player in turn, two threes and then one two. The remainder of the pack is placed on the table face downwards, and the top card is exposed and placed beside it. As before, the object of the game is to arrange one's hand in groups of three of a kind or sequences of three or more of a suit. Upon the deal being completed the player on the left of the dealer may take either the exposed card or a card from the top of the pack, and discard a card from his hand, this being placed on the exposed card at the side of the pack. A hand dealt may be:

♥ 9, J ♣ 8, K, J
♦ 8 ♠ 7, 8

The player can immediately arrange the three 8s as three of a kind, and, ignoring the exposed card (the 5 of Hearts), which is of no use to him, he will draw the top card of the pack—which may prove to be the 10 of Hearts. This he can place with the 9 and J, giving him 9, 10, J of Hearts as a Sequence. He will now discard the 7 of Spades and his hand after the operation will be three 8s, 9, 10, J of Hearts; and K, J of Clubs. Upon the pack coming round to him again, after being used by all the other players, he will be trying to obtain either another 8 to add to his three, or the Q of Hearts; and he will discard either the K or J of Clubs. When the hand has been so arranged that the whole of it fits in threes or sequences, and the odd cards are not more than two, totalling in pips not more than seven, the player declares "Rummy" and places his hand on the table, while the other players may, from their odd cards, add to his threes and sequences. Thus, if a "Rummy" hand is:

three 8s, 9, 10, J of Hearts; and two odd cards—
say 3 of Diamonds and 4 of Spades—

the other players may add their eights to his and also the 8 or Q of Hearts. If one player adds the Q another may add the K and so on. The winner is paid for the number of pips on the cards of the other players which do not fit in their own hand, after deducting the score of the odd cards of the player calling " Rummy."

Thus, a player with a hand of three 7s, 8, 10 J of Spades ; K, Q of Hearts, may add the 8 to the Rummy hand, and the K, Q of Hearts, and is then left with the 10 and J of Spades, scoring 20 (court cards count 10, Ace 1) from which he deducts the 7 of the Rummy hand and pays 13. The deuces are considered as Jokers and may be used in place of any card. Thus, 2 sevens and a deuce count as three 7s, and deuce, 9, 10 as a sequence of 8, 9, 10 or 9, 10, J.

Three Jokers are included when playing with two packs, and any player being dealt three Jokers receives 12 counters from each player, and 6 counters for 2 Jokers, or 3 for one. Players having each one Joker do not pay each other. Deuces when dealt to a player are not Jokers for this purpose.

The game may end at any time, players being paid for the counters in their possession according to the rate at which they were purchased. Thus, if 48 counters were purchased for twopence, a player with 36 counters receives three-halfpence. Counters may be purchased at any rate of value determined before play commences. Millionaires, one presumes, play with counters purchased at ten shillings each ; in the more modest family circles 48 counters for twopence is more usual—and quite sufficient to give the game the necessary " kick."

Another method of scoring is to write on a score pad against each players' name the total of the pips he holds instead of paying counters to the winner. These scores are carried forward after each deal until one player reaches 100 and then he is considered to be out of the game, and the remaining players carry on until all are eliminated except one—who is the winner.

A further variation is to allow the player going out of the game to re-enter by paying an agreed stake of one penny (or one shilling or whatever it may be), and he re-enters at the highest score of the remaining players. Thus if the scores are 45, 64, 75, 86, a player reaching 100 may, upon paying his stake, re-enter at 86.

The game ends when all the players, except one, exceed 100 in one hand, the remaining player, who, of course, has scored less than 100, being the winner. If the scores are, for instance, 94, 96, 98 and 92, and the player with 92 calls "Rummy," should the scores on that hand, when added to the scores of 94, 96 and 98 force these players to a score exceeding 100, the game ends and the player with 92 is the winner, taking all the stakes previously paid for re-entry. No player may call "Rummy" if his odd card, added to his score totals or exceeds 100. Thus a player with a score of 97 cannot call Rummy until his odd cards total less than three.

If the whole pack has been exhausted, and no player has called Rummy, the pack is reversed and the procedure continued.

PRINTED IN ENGLAND BY MARDON, SON AND HALL, BRISTOL,
BRANCH OF THE IMPERIAL TOBACCO CO. (OF GREAT BRITAIN AND IRELAND), LTD.